HAUNTED CANADA 10

MORE SCARY TRUE STORIES

JOEL A.
SUTHERLAND

Illustrations by
Mark Savona

Scholastic Canada Ltd.
Toronto New York London Auckland Sydney
Mexico City New Delhi Hong Kong Buenos Aires

Scholastic Canada Ltd.
604 King Street West, Toronto, Ontario M5V 1E1, Canada

Scholastic Inc.
557 Broadway, New York, NY 10012, USA

Scholastic Australia Pty Limited
PO Box 579, Gosford, NSW 2250, Australia

Scholastic New Zealand Limited
Private Bag 94407, Botany, Manukau 2163, New Zealand

Scholastic Children's Books
Euston House, 24 Eversholt Street, London NW1 1DB, UK

www.scholastic.ca

Library and Archives Canada Cataloguing in Publication

Title: Haunted Canada 10 : more scary true stories / Joel A. Sutherland ;
illustrations by Mark Savona.
Other titles: Haunted Canada ten
Names: Sutherland, Joel A., 1980- author. | Savona, Mark, illustrator.
Identifiers: Canadiana (print) 20190215437 | Canadiana (ebook) 20190215445 |
ISBN 9781443175784 (softcover) | ISBN 9781443175791 (ebook)
Subjects: LCSH: Ghosts—Canada—Juvenile literature. | LCSH: Haunted
places—Canada—Juvenile literature.
Classification: LCC BF1472.C3 S987 2020 | DDC j133.10971—dc23

Photos ©: Cover photo © Shutterstock.com; 4: Frederic Ansermoz/IBuyPhotos.
com; 13: Courtesy CKUA Radio; 17: Courtesy of Joseph Brant Museum; 35:
courtesy of Deena Vallieres; 48: University of Saskatchewan, University Archives
and Special Collections, Hugh "Howdy" McPhail fonds, MG 402, Town Series 2,
Bickleigh, SK.; 69: Lembi Buchanan/Dreamstime; 77: University of Manitoba
Archives & Special Collections, Hamilton Family fonds PC 12 (A1979-041), Box
9, Envelope VII, #28d; 100: Coll-137 2.07.012 Houses, St John's, Sutherland
Place. Archives and Special Collections, Queen Elizabeth II Library, Memorial
University; 111: John Mahler/Getty Images.

6 5 4 3 2 1   Printed in Canada   139   20 21 22 23 24

For you, dear reader.
Ten volumes! Seven written by yours
truly, and I'm incredibly proud of each
and every one. I wouldn't have made
it here without your support. My
eternal thanks to you.

INTRODUCTION

When I wrote *Haunted Canada 4*, my first foray into the series that Pat Hancock kicked off, I never imagined I'd someday be writing an introduction for the tenth volume. And yet, six years later, here we are. As I've researched, written and edited this book, I've been in a perpetual state of mild shock, like waking up and realizing your dream was actually your reality. But despite the shock I feel at having reached this particular milestone, it shouldn't be a surprise to me or anyone who knows me that my life has led me here.

I've always loved storytelling and have long had a particular fondness for tales filled to the brim with things that go bump in the night. *Haunted Canada 4* wasn't the first time I profited from spinning a creepy yarn. That goes back farther in time — back to the summer between Grades 5 and 6. I was at a sleepover with two friends, and as midnight approached, one of us (Can you guess who?) suggested we take turns telling scary stories.

My friends did an admirable job telling genuinely creepy tales. So when it came to my turn, I knew I'd need to step things up a notch. The specifics of the story are lost in time — I'm relatively certain it involved a hitch-hiker and a broken-down car, or a bathroom mirror and a deadly curse, or a this-call-is-coming-from-within-the-house-style twist, or . . . something. I spoke with an eerie voice, I jolted my audience with chilling sound effects and I paused for dramatic effect whenever the tension mounted. It shouldn't have worked, it should have been cheesy and over-the-top, but when I finally reached THE END and took a deep breath, one of my friends reached into his pocket, pulled out a dollar, and placed it in my hand.

"What's this for?" I asked.

"That," he said in a whisper, "is for telling the scariest story I have ever heard."

I was hooked. I could scare people! I knew I'd found my calling.

Which brings us to *Haunted Canada 10*. In the following pages you'll find something to petrify every palate. Ghosts that lurk in bedroom closets and spirits that attack the living in broad daylight. Haunted houses, forts, hockey arenas and abandoned asylums. Stories from the past and stories from the present. You'll even find a grinning head . . . with no body.

Will one of these stories be the scariest one *you* have ever heard? There's only one way to find out. Work up some courage, brace yourself, and turn the page. There have been nine prior volumes in the series, so you should know by now what you're getting yourself into. And if this is your first taste of Haunted Canada, don't say I didn't warn you.

Frightfully yours,

NIGHTTIME IN THE ASYLUM

Sainte-Clotilde-de-Horton, Quebec

Four brave men and women stood on the steps of the abandoned asylum and wondered what awaited them within the large, imposing building. As members of APPA Paranormal, they would go on to investigate the Sainte-Clotilde-de-Horton Asylum more than fifteen times between 2006 and 2017, but their first visit was easily one of the most memorable. After months of planning, they were happy and excited that the day had come when they'd finally set foot inside. But Patrick Sabourin, one of the group's founders, was also overcome by a profound sadness. The building had a lot of history and had seen no shortage of tragedy.

Originally built in 1939 as a monastery for the Fathers of the Sacred Heart, the building was briefly used as the novitiate of the Brothers of Christian Instruction in the 1950s. On Christmas Day, 1959, three students died when they accidentally set a fire. The building was purchased by the government in the 1960s and converted into an asylum for people with intellectual disabilities. In 1988 a patient set a fire in a central dormitory on the top floor, killing nine people.

It's believed some of the twelve souls who died in the two separate fires have remained in the asylum long after it was closed and fell into disrepair.

Patrick led his team — his wife and co-founder, Izabel Descheneaux, technical director Éric Chicoine and mental health worker Marie Josée Lamoureux — inside. Entering the asylum was like stepping into a nightmare. Just about every window was broken and boarded up. The walls were crumbling and covered in graffiti and mould. The ceiling had many holes and looked like it might come down at any moment. The floor was covered in trash and puddles of dirty brown water. Old, broken furniture had been left behind to rot. They passed an inscription that read "*Sinite parvulos venire ad me*," which translates to "Let the children come to me."

During his research, Patrick had uncovered several reports from people who had heard voices in the halls and screams behind walls. Some of those people had also seen ghosts drifting among the shadows. Now, seeing the inside of the building for himself, he wasn't surprised. There was no chance the asylum *wasn't* haunted. More than that — judging by its appearance and the sombre feeling that hung in the air as thick as smoke, it might have been the most haunted building in the province.

Not much time passed before the ghosts revealed themselves to the group. Although they were alone, laughter cut through the silence — laughter that soon turned to crying. Patrick and the others paused and held their breath, trying not to make a sound, waiting for what they might hear next.

"Where are you going?" a soft voice asked.

Patrick was too shocked to answer. They moved deeper into the building, then descended into the depths of the basement.

"Help me," a young voice said, full of sadness and fear. It sounded too close for comfort.

One of the members took a picture of the empty room. Later, when reviewing what they had captured, they saw a small boy holding out his hand. His expression was full of sorrow and pain. Although the boy only revealed himself in a picture, two other horrifying spirits appeared in person.

The first was the misty form of a human that flew past them like the wind and floated up the stairs. The second was an incredibly tall man who approached Izabel when she was alone. She turned and ran as quickly as she could, refusing to wait and see what the tall man wanted.

A few years later, in 2009, Roger Thivierge and Marie-Claude Martineau purchased the forty-three-hectare property, abandoned asylum and all. The couple thought it would be the ideal retirement project. Their plan was to start a French bulldog breeding business and raise funds to convert the asylum into a seniors' residence. They didn't know they had purchased a haunted building, but they soon found out.

Within weeks, trespassing ghost hunters began to sneak onto their property late at night. Some were more destructive than others, breaking windows and damaging walls. Roger and Marie-Claude put up homemade signs that read "*Privé*." But the signs were largely ignored, and one was written over with spray paint to read "THE DEVIL IS HERE." Once their patience had completely run out, Roger and Marie-Claude called the police. One of the officers made an off-the-cuff suggestion: Why not cash in on the macabre interest and charge people a fee to visit the haunted asylum?

A hallway in the Sainte-Clotilde-de-Horton Asylum

The next time someone showed up to sneak onto the grounds, the couple stopped them and said they could tour the building . . . for a price. The visitor eagerly paid up. Word spread, and before long people were travelling from across the province, the country and even the world, with visitors from as far away as Europe and South America.

Patrick, Izabel and other members of APPA Paranormal returned to the site many times over the years, and they were never disappointed. But in 2017 the local fire department deemed the building unsafe, and the municipality ordered a fence to be installed around the building to keep people out. During their last visit before this happened, Patrick and Izabel spoke with not one, not two, but *three* different ghosts. Each spirit was creepier than the last.

First, they went to the basement. They thought they could hear something in the shadows and had a feeling they were no longer alone.

"What's your name?" Patrick asked the darkness.

"James," a young boy answered. It was the same voice they had heard many years before.

Although Patrick and Izabel were scared, they also laughed a little. To make contact with a ghost was the reason they had visited, after all. Soon they went back up to the main floor, where they heard the second voice.

As they entered a dark room, they could hear someone snickering. It sounded like another child, but this one was a girl. Izabel asked what the girl's name was.

"Amélie," she yelled, making Patrick and Izabel nearly jump out of their skin. They moved on, eventually reaching the top floor.

Standing in the centre of the dormitory where the fire that killed nine people took place, Patrick and Izabel tried to encourage the ghosts to come out of the woodwork. But nothing happened. That was odd, since the rest of the building had always been so active.

"If you don't talk to me, I will leave," Patrick finally said. He and Izabel began walking back to the staircase but were interrupted by the third voice of the night.

"Hey, where are you going?" a man's voice boomed.

Despite their fear, Patrick and Izabel managed to hold their ground and speak a little more with the ghost. He identified himself as Gerard, which was the name of one of the people who had died in the fire. Although Gerard seemed to want them to stay, Patrick and Izabel soon left and stepped back out into the moonlight. Although they were excited by all of the incredible activity they had experienced, they were also a little relieved to have left the asylum without suffering any physical harm.

But it's often the psychological harm that cuts the deepest, and in a place like the Sainte-Clotilde-de-Horton Asylum, maladies of the mind have a habit of lingering . . . sometimes long after death.

SOMETHING IN THE CLOSET

Burnaby, British Columbia

Ann Nelson adored her home. She had moved into the house on Georgia Street in 1965 with her husband and three children. They thought they'd never leave. The yard was nice and big, with plenty of space for all the children to run around and play. There was a peach tree that grew the largest, most delicious peaches Ann had ever tasted. The neighbours were all friendly and gave the street a sense of safety and community. It was a dream house, practically perfect in every way, except one. But that one problem wasn't something small, like being located on a busy street, or fixable, like a leaky faucet or squeaky floorboards.

Something dwelled in the darkness of Ann's son's closet.

"Mom," Jim said, walking into his parents' room early one morning, "there was something in my room last night."

7

Ann sat up in bed and asked her son what he was talking about.

Jim had heard something moving in his closet but he had been too frightened to investigate. He had fallen back asleep once the noise stopped but was woken again a little later when someone sat down on the edge of his bed. When he looked to see who was there, he was shocked to find his room completely empty, but there was a depression in his bedding.

Ann dismissed her son's concerns and told him he'd had a nightmare. A vivid one, maybe, and a scary one, certainly, but just a nightmare.

Two months later Ann experienced her own nighttime terror that forced her to reconsider what she'd told her son.

She was lying in bed one night, not yet asleep, when she spotted a tall, blond-haired man with piercing blue eyes standing in her bedroom doorway. He had materialized as if out of thin air and wore an angry expression. But what concerned and terrified Ann more than anything was the gun he pointed straight at her. She quickly woke her husband, and the stranger vanished without a trace. The couple got out of bed and thoroughly searched the house but found no sign of the man or of a forced entry. All of the evidence seemed to point to the fact that the man wasn't of the living, breathing variety, but Ann wouldn't allow herself to fully believe that. Not yet.

Two weeks later the man appeared in the middle of the night once more. This time he was dressed in a blue suit and white shirt, but what was most striking about his appearance was the glowing halo floating in the air above his head. It was enough to convince Ann that the man, whoever he was, was a ghost. But that was the last time he was seen for some time. And life, as it has a habit of doing (even when living in a haunted house), returned to normal — until Ann's mother came for an extended visit.

Early one morning, a week before her mother would return home, mother and daughter were enjoying some coffee at the breakfast table when, out of the blue, Ann's mother made an odd admission.

"Annie, I have something to tell you. I don't want to scare you, but there have been a few times here I felt someone sitting on my bed. And something was in the closet."

Although it was a warm, sunny day, a shiver ran up Ann's back. Her mother had been sleeping in Jim's room, and what she'd described — both the mattress being depressed as if someone was sitting on it and the unshakable feeling that something was hiding in the closet — perfectly mirrored her son's claims.

Later that night, Ann told her husband she no longer wanted to live in that house. It was far too creepy. He agreed, and they put the house up for sale as soon as they could. It sold within a month — not surprising considering how charming it was — and Ann's family moved into another house in Burnaby.

Time passed and Ann was happy with the decision they'd made, but she still missed the house — ghost or no ghost. A year after they'd moved, she and her husband returned to the neighbourhood to attend a small gathering of old friends and neighbours. Over coffee, one of their friends mentioned that all of them had been surprised by the sudden move. Ann had never told any of her neighbours the reason. Where would she have begun? And who would have believed her?

But that day Ann let her guard down and finally admitted they'd moved out of their dream home because it was haunted.

To be expected, all of their friends were shocked by the news, but one was more shocked than the others.

"It was my brother who used to live there, but he's gone now," one of the men said. "He was killed in a head-on collision."

Ann had to ask. "Do you have a photograph of your brother?"

The man did. He stepped out of the room and returned a short while later holding a picture of eleven men that had been taken the night before his brother died. He didn't point out which of the men was his brother. He didn't need to.

Ann took one quick glance at the photograph and pointed at a tall man with blond hair and blue eyes. "That's him. That's the ghost."

Ann felt better than ever about their decision to move. No house — regardless of the big yard or the delicious peaches — is worth living in disharmony with a ghost.

HAUNT THE BLOCK

Edmonton, Alberta

In 2009 a summer intern working at CKUA Radio, then located in an old building called Alberta Block, got more than the work experience she had hoped for. A lot more.

She was the only person working in the dark, dank basement when she suddenly had the feeling that she wasn't alone. She was cataloguing records on a computer in the back corner of the room, and by quitting time she was eager to leave both the basement and the building. She turned off the computer, stood up, and crossed the room to pick up her keys from the spot she'd left them.

But her keys were no longer there. She'd placed them near the edge of a desk by the door, and now they were gone. Maybe they'd fallen off the desk. She checked the floor, but the keys weren't there. Maybe she'd made a mistake and left them somewhere else. Even though she was fairly certain that wasn't the case, she left the basement and retraced her steps, searching the building high and low. No luck.

When she returned to the basement, frustrated and annoyed, she finally found her keys. They were sitting near the edge of the desk, right where she'd left them. Right where they had *not* been a short while before.

Another day soon after, the intern — characterized by CKUA chief executive officer Ken Regan as very intelligent and not easily frightened — was again working alone in the basement. She left her keys in the same place, on the same desk, thinking there was no reason anything odd would happen to them again, but she was wrong.

As she worked at the computer, the keys flew off the table and hit the floor with a clatter. She spun around, but there was no one there — no one she could see, anyway.

"Stop it!" she yelled to the empty room.

It worked. That was the last time she ever had an encounter with Alberta Block's resident ghost.

Over the years Alberta Block has striven to be a connection space for art, commerce and entertainment. Built on Jasper Avenue in the early 1900s, it has housed a variety of businesses, including a piano maker, a beauty salon, a dressmaker, lawyers, a photo studio and a digital arts college. But the longest-running tenant was CKUA Radio. And although the station moved to a new location in 2012, one of its former employees has refused to move on, despite the fact that he died in the 1970s.

Sam, the building's caretaker, was described by

co-workers as polite, quiet and strange. He was a big man. He never laughed, but he loved to sing as he swept the floors, and he smoked a pipe or cigar at all hours of the day. His quiet disposition hid a checkered past; it was said that Sam had had ties to a terrorist organization and that he had once threatened the life of Alberta premier Ernest Manning. For this crime Sam had been lobotomized, a surgical procedure that severs connections in the brain's prefrontal cortex. This would explain why his co-workers found Sam to be very quiet and more than a little strange.

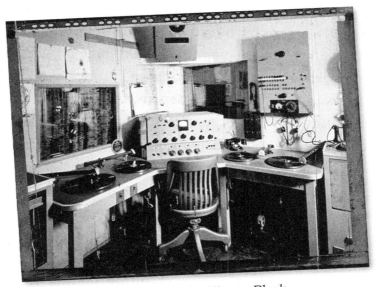

The studio of CKUA Radio in Alberta Block

Since Sam's death in the 1970s, employees have heard him singing from across empty rooms. Like the summer intern whose keys were thrown off the desk, others have felt unseen eyes watching them from the shadows, particularly in the basement.

One night a tape machine broke, and Larry King, a

technician, had to take it to the basement to repair it. The tape machine was heavy and difficult to carry. As he struggled down the stairs, Larry was suddenly overcome with the odd but certain sensation that he was not alone. His skin prickled as a shiver danced up and down his spine. He paused and glanced around. When he had confirmed that there was no one within sight, he carried on.

Once he had reached the bottom of the stairs, he turned around and went to hip check the crash bar to force the door open without using his hands. But as he attempted to do so, the door flew open all on its own and Larry nearly fell to the floor. He managed to regain his balance, but if he had fallen, the tape machine would have landed on top of him, crushing the poor technician.

Sam wouldn't remain hidden from sight for long. Bill Coull, a long-time employee of the radio station, was in the control room an hour past midnight. Bill was alone . . . but he had the sinking sensation that he wasn't. He felt a presence. When Bill happened to look at the control-room window, he saw the reflection of a face that wasn't his own. The lighting was dim but he could clearly make out a pair of eyes and bright white teeth with a cigar clenched between them. Someone was standing behind him, but when Bill spun around there was no one there. And when he looked at the glass again, the reflection was gone.

Although CKUA no longer broadcasts from Alberta Block, Sam is still on the air — or rather, *in* the air. You might not be able to see him, but you'll definitely be able to sense him.

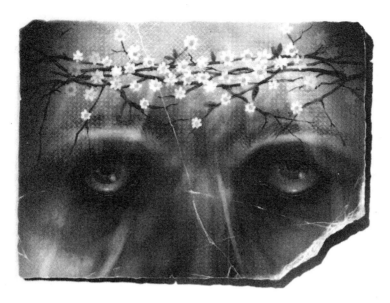

WHERE EVIL DWELLS

Burlington, Ontario

Terry Boyle wandered through the Joseph Brant Museum looking for Eliza. He walked from room to room hoping to find her hiding in a corner or lurking in the shadows. On the second floor, Terry lingered in a small room that housed a glass display case, waiting and watching. He took many pictures of the case — not for the historical artifacts it contained, but for something else. He hoped to catch sight of Eliza reflected in the glass.

Terry, an author and lecturer on Canadian history and folklore, had spoken to people who reported feeling terrified of those display cases, far too terrified to even walk near them. On one occasion, Barbara Teatero, the museum director, reported finding two women with their hands pressed against the glass, staring intently at something in the reflection only they could see. When Barbara approached them and asked if she could help, one of the women informed her in an ominous tone that there were ghosts in the museum.

Terry took a few more pictures, but when Eliza didn't appear he moved on. His search led him up the narrow staircase at the back of the second-floor hallway and into the dusty attic. As soon as he set foot in the attic, Terry was overcome with the unshakable feeling that he wasn't alone.

Eliza was there. Terry couldn't see her, but he knew it beyond a shadow of a doubt.

Scanning the attic and taking in all of the items that had been stored there, Terry recalled another story Barbara had shared with him. She'd been working on the third floor with her sister, carefully packing costumes and period clothing into cardboard boxes. Without warning, one of the boxes flew into the air and struck Barbara's sister on the shoulder. It was as if it had been thrown by invisible hands.

Would something fly through the air and strike Terry as he wandered around the third floor? If he was concerned by that possibility, he didn't let his nerves get the better of him. Instead he tried to imagine what life had been like at the turn of the eighteenth century when Burlington's first citizen settled in the area.

Joseph Brant, or Thayendanegea, a Kanyen'kehà:ka (Mohawk) war chief and British army captain, was granted 3,450 acres of land by King George III in 1798 for his service during the Seven Years War and the American

Revolution. Brant built his home near where the museum stands today, and he died there in 1807.

Nearly seventy years later, the estate was sold and the property was turned into the Hotel Brant. Then in 1917 the hotel was expropriated by the government for use as a soldiers' hospital. The hotel was boarded up and its rooms remodelled to serve as wards and operating rooms. After the remaining soldiers were transferred elsewhere in the 1930s, the hotel was abandoned, vandalized and partially destroyed by fire. A replica of the historic house was opened in 1942 and has since operated as the Joseph Brant Museum.

The first report of the Brant property being haunted predates the hotel. A neighbouring farmer reported to the *American Historical Record* in 1873 that ghosts dwelled

Joseph Brant Museum display as it appeared in 2014

within Brant's original house. In 1891 the skeleton of a large man was discovered buried on the grounds. And in an article that appeared in the *Hamilton Spectator*, reporter Michael Bennett claimed that the supernatural heart of the museum beat within the attic — the very attic where Terry stood alone, thinking back on the property's past and some of the ghost stories he'd heard.

He took a few more pictures of the room where he felt Eliza's presence, waited for something to happen, and then when nothing out of the ordinary occurred, walked back down to the second floor.

He passed the room with the glass display case and turned into the room across the hall. It was a larger room, but that's not what had drawn Terry to it. It happened to be the room with the most compelling ghost stories ever reported.

In 1987 a woman was there for a meeting that began at 8 p.m. At approximately 9:30 p.m. the woman was overcome by a sense — a sixth sense — that something evil was nearby. Her gaze was drawn to the doorway. And there she was — Eliza, the museum's ghost. She was wearing a long, white, old-fashioned wedding dress with long sleeves, and her face was obscured by a veil. She had dark brown hair and was exceptionally thin. No one else appeared to be able to see her, but Eliza locked eyes with the woman and spoke in a hushed voice.

"My name is Eliza," she said. "I was born in England in 1847. Don't let my appearance fool you, because things are not what they seem."

And then she disappeared into thin air.

The woman was so terrified by what she'd seen and what Eliza had said that she had to flee from the building immediately.

Once that story spread, Ann Urquhart, the museum's volunteer coordinator, decided to leave a tape recorder running after the museum had closed for the night. Although she might not have thought she'd actually collect any conclusive evidence, Ann could hardly believe her own ears when she played the tape back the following morning. She heard, among other sounds, papers rustling, coins being dropped on a table, and doors opening and closing.

When Terry entered the room where Eliza had been seen in her wedding dress, an old man was there cataloguing the museum's small library. Terry happened to spot a book he had written in 1979. Thinking he'd take a quick look at it, he reached up and placed his hand on it, but he wasn't able to pull it off the shelf. Instead, it flew off on its own, along with three other books. Those three crashed to the floor, but Terry's book sailed through the air and struck the old man on the side of the head, knocking his glasses off and sending the spectacles into the hall.

Terry's immediate concern was for the man. He hoped he wasn't hurt. He picked up the glasses and returned them to the man, then apologized and tried to explain what had happened. But the man didn't believe a word. How could he? It was preposterous to claim that the book had flown through the air on its own, but Terry knew that was exactly what had happened. And it had happened quickly and with incredible force. Just as he'd known Eliza had been with him in the attic, Terry knew that she had followed him to the second floor and was responsible for throwing his book.

Terry also knew that Eliza was an evil presence.

He thanked her for making an appearance and quickly left the museum. Eliza remained and shows no signs of ever leaving.

THE HAUNTING OF BIBLE HILL

Bible Hill, Nova Scotia

Lucy Langille and Rachel Hull, sisters whose husbands were both across the Atlantic Ocean fighting in World War II, were passing a peaceful evening in the company of Arnold, Lucy's sixteen-year-old son, and June, Rachel's twelve-year-old daughter. It was December 1941 and the four family members shared a modest house on Farnham Road, a quiet street in the west end of Bible Hill, an equally quiet village northeast of the town of Truro. But the peace and quiet of the night was about to be broken.

A sound came from a nearby closet. The family stopped talking and fell silent. The closet door creaked open on its own. The sisters and their children held their breath. Time seemed to slow down. And then a pair of shoes stepped into the light. Everyone screamed and jumped out of their chairs. The shoes weren't worn by a man or a woman — not even by a child. They were worn by no one. They walked across the floor — *clomp, clomp, clomp* — as the family watched in horror.

Unfortunately for Lucy, Rachel and their kids, it wasn't an isolated incident, but rather the beginning of nearly constant paranormal events that would take place in their house over the coming months. Inanimate objects were moved or thrown by some unseen presence. Pots and pans rattled on the stove, and cutlery, a clock and a fireplace poker sailed through the air, nearly injuring people on more than one occasion.

By the spring of 1942, the sisters were nearing their breaking point and needed some comfort, or at least some reassurance that they weren't losing their minds, so they told a group of friends from the neighbourhood what they'd been dealing with. Their friends didn't believe them. Flying objects and shoes that walked across rooms on their own? Surely Lucy and Rachel were joking. So the sisters invited their friends over to see for themselves. The friends accepted. If nothing else, it would be a chance for all of them to get together.

However, Lucy and Rachel made everyone split up shortly after they arrived. The paranormal activity had taken place throughout the house, so they'd be more likely to encounter something if they weren't all congregated in one area. Every light was turned off — darkness would be best to entice the ghosts to materialize — and flashlights were distributed to everyone. And then the group waited for something to happen.

They didn't need to wait long.

Creak, creak, creak.

"What's that?" one of the neighbours asked.

Lucy recognized the sound immediately. "It's the ghost rocking in the other room," she said.

With their flashlights gripped tightly, everyone rushed into the room. Beams of light scanned the room and fell upon a single rocking chair in the corner. It was rocking back and forth vigorously, but no one was in it. A quick search of the room determined it was empty, and yet there was no other way in or out.

There must have been an explanation. "Somebody made it rock by pulling a black thread or horsehairs tied together," one of the neighbours assured the group as the chair slowly stopped rocking. "Look for a thread."

Everyone looked, but no such thread was found.

Another guest claimed that someone in the basement might be moving the chair by sliding a magnet along the bottom of the floorboards. They searched the chair for any type of metal, but it was made completely of wood.

The neighbours still didn't believe a ghost had been involved — they hadn't actually seen the chair begin to rock, after all — so they addressed the "ghost" directly: either rock the chair again as they watched it closely, or prove to everyone that no such ghost was in the house.

The chair rocked.

Hastily, everyone fled the room and regrouped in the kitchen. Before anyone could object, one of the neighbours asked if there was also a ghost in that part of the house.

Scriiitch!

Something scraped across a wooden shelf. Everyone shone their lights at the source of the sound. It was a milk bottle, sliding across the shelf on its own. But there was no time to investigate — the kitchen was about to descend into chaos.

Thwack!

A window blind rolled up all on its own.

Slam!

The kitchen table flipped over.

Thud!

A drawer rocketed open and the cutlery from within levitated into the air.

Clatter!

All of the cutlery fell to the ground.

Crash!

A tin lunch box flew off a hook on the wall and hit the floor more than three metres away.

The neighbours had been wrong. Lucy and Rachel's house was haunted, and the ghosts were no friends to the living. The neighbours gladly returned to the safety of their own homes and word of what they had experienced on Farnham Road quickly spread far and wide.

Curious onlookers drove slowly up and down the street, trying to see if they could spot anything unusual from outside. And when George Hanebury and Earl Talbot, two local photographers, and John Murphy, the editor of the *Truro Daily News*, heard that a local home was haunted, they smelled a story and paid a visit.

Eager for more people to believe them, Lucy and Rachel were happy to welcome the men into their home. The family, photographers and editor went straight to the kitchen. It was, after all, the location of the majority of the activity. Not too long after George and Earl had set up their cameras, the drawer once more flew open. But this time, instead of simply levitating and then crashing to the floor, the cutlery flew through the air and pierced the far wall. One knife impaled the wood centimetres from John's head.

Unfortunately the photographers hadn't been prepared for anything to happen so quickly. But they were ready the next time. A heavy iron on the stove began to shake violently. Young June, who'd been standing closest to the stove, backed away from the sound in terror. Despite the fear they felt, George and Earl both managed to take a picture. Unable to wait until morning, the men developed their photographs that very night. Captured in one of the two photographs was the image of an adult's hand gripping the iron as it shook. But none of the adults had been anywhere near the iron and no one had seen anyone gripping it.

The articles they later published in the *Truro Daily News* were picked up by papers across the country. Oddly enough, that was the last time the ghosts of Bible Hill haunted Lucy and Rachel's home. No one knows why. Perhaps, like the sisters who needed to convince their friends that their house truly was haunted, the spirits needed to convince the country that they truly existed.

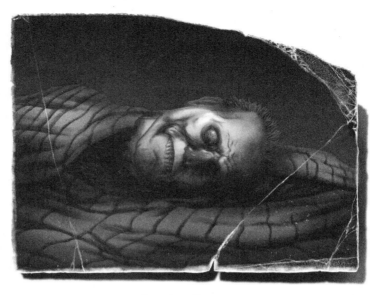

THE GRINNING HEAD

Swan Island, Newfoundland and Labrador

The group of kayakers couldn't believe their luck. They were bone tired from exploring the Bay of Exploits all day by the time they reached Swan Island. Just when they thought they would need to spend the night camping under the stars, they happened upon a cabin. They knocked on the door. No one answered. They opened the door and called out. Still no one answered. They explored each of the cabin's small rooms. It was empty and there were no signs that anyone had been there recently. The prospect of getting a good night's sleep, protected from the elements, was too appealing to pass up, so they decided they'd spend the night inside and carry on in the morning.

There was plenty of space, so they decided to spread out and each sleep in their own room. But getting a good night's sleep wasn't in the cards. Certainly not that night, and not for many nights thereafter.

One of the men woke up in the middle of the night. At first he didn't know what had roused him, but then he felt something odd. His sleeping bag was wet. Was there a leak in the roof? Had he had an accident? He examined his sleeping bag a little closer — it was hard to see in the darkness — and discovered the liquid hadn't come from a leak or a full bladder.

It was blood.

Was it his own? As he started to check his body for injuries, something caught his eye. Something round, roughly the size of a basketball, rested at the bottom of his sleeping bag near his feet.

It was a human head.

He stared at it, frozen in shock, and then the head grinned at him.

The man screamed, far louder than he ever would have imagined possible.

The rest of the group woke immediately and rushed to the man's room to see what was the matter, but by the time they had arrived both the blood and the grinning head had vanished without a trace. Unsurprisingly, the man couldn't fall back asleep that night. As soon as the sun peeked over the horizon, the group packed up, returned to their kayaks, and put Swan Island — and the grinning head — behind them.

European settlers arrived at Swan Island in the 1880s and established a small fishing community on the south shore, but a nearby Beothuk burial ground points to earlier use. Swan Island, along with Little Berry Island and Long Island, formed a natural shelter for ships, making it an ideal area for fishermen. There was plenty of cod, herring, salmon and lobster, but by 1948 most of the families who once called Swan Island home had moved on, and the island was largely abandoned.

It might be abandoned, but it's far from quiet. People have reported hearing ships moving across the empty harbour, as if some of the deceased fishermen are still hard at work. Other people who have camped on the island have woken in the morning to discover their tightly tied knots have been undone and their boats have drifted far away. A man who was camping on the island overnight with his dog didn't get a moment of shut-eye; the canine sensed some unseen presence and spent the entire night growling with his hackles raised. And others claim to have seen a mysterious figure walking through the woods; sometimes all that is seen of the figure is its floating face.

But none of these reports are nearly as disturbing as the kayaker who woke one night and came face to face with the grinning head. There have been many accounts of headless ghosts spotted across the country, but in terms of creepiness, the bodiless ghost of Swan Island is ahead of them all.

ORDEAL BY FIRE

Port Perry, Ontario

Shortly after Whitney and Mark Freeman purchased a restaurant in downtown Port Perry, their dog went wild. The couple watched in shock as the dog ran full speed through the kitchen, down the back hall, and out onto the glassed-in porch that was used as an additional dining area. The canine, who was normally very well behaved, stopped at table thirteen and began to bark loudly. But no one was seated there.

At the time, the Freemans had no idea what to think. They hadn't yet heard the ghost stories.

Constructed in 1913 as a private residence, the building needed some work, so Mark had the entire building rewired. But whatever dwelled in the walls decided to do its own electrical work.

Mark and Whitney were relaxing one night, watching the sun set through the window and enjoying the peaceful evening, when the lights suddenly turned on. From then on, the light switch in that room was reversed — flipping the switch down would turn the light on and flipping it up would turn it off. This happened one by one to every single light in the house. An electrician was called in but had no idea how each switch had, well, *switched* without human interference. The Freemans were annoyed. They'd soon become terrified.

The second floor, above the restaurant, was the Freemans' living quarters, which included a bedroom, a small office, a living room and a door to the attic. One day Mark noticed the attic door was open. The door had a deadbolt on it and the couple were very careful to make sure it was always shut and locked. Mark thought it was strange to find the door open but figured it was a simple oversight. He closed the door, locked it, and walked away. Three seconds after he'd locked the door, it swung open again. The evidence was quickly mounting, and as difficult as it was to believe, neither Mark nor Whitney could ignore it: the restaurant was haunted.

Whitney and Mark needed a vacation, but since one of them had to remain at home to run the restaurant, they decided to go on separate trips one after the other. The night before Whitney returned and Mark left, he was walking down the stairs to the basement when he suddenly issued a warning to the ghost.

"I'm going away for a couple of days," he said to the surrounding darkness, "and I know that you like to disturb

Whitney. I don't want you to do anything while I'm away." And then, in his sternest voice possible, he added, "Is that understood?"

As soon as he had finished speaking, all of the basement lights turned on.

It seemed to be a sign of agreement. At least that's how Mark took it. But either the ghost had turned on the lights to signify something else, or it never intended to keep its promise.

One night while she was alone, Whitney was woken in the middle of the night. She'd been in a deep sleep, but she heard someone call her name as clear as a bell. It was a woman's voice, and her presence was so thick in the bedroom that Whitney could *feel* her there.

A few nights later, Whitney was once again woken in the middle of the night.

Rattle-rattle-clank!

It was the sound of her pet rabbit's water bottle. She kept the cage in her bedroom, and the bottle, which was attached to the metal bars, made a horrible racket whenever the rabbit took a drink. Often when this woke Whitney, she'd get up to refill the bottle. So that night, just as she'd done countless nights before, Whitney got out of bed to fill the bottle. It wasn't until she crossed the room that she remembered the rabbit was spending a few days up north with a family member. Not only was there no rabbit in the room, but there was no cage and no water bottle. Whitney couldn't help but wonder if the rabbit had always been responsible for rattling the bottle, or if something else was to blame.

In 1986 Whitney and Mark sold the restaurant to Niki Bainbridge, who named it Murray House. Although the ghost had never appeared before the Freemans, Niki, who moved in with her children, wouldn't be quite so lucky. She often saw a woman in her seventies who wore old-fashioned clothing: a long white apron over a high-collared blue dress. Whenever Niki came face to face with her, the old woman would smile at Niki and then pass through a wall. This was the first ghost Niki would see in the house, but she was far from the last.

One night while asleep in her attic bedroom, she was woken by the sound of someone else breathing deeply. Startled, she quickly turned on a light and couldn't believe what she saw. Lying next to her was a person with his or her back to her. Niki had no idea what to do, but after a second or two the stranger slowly disappeared and the indentation in the mattress where he or she had been lying returned to its regular flat shape.

Another night an unknown voice shouted Niki's name directly into her ear as she was about to fall asleep, but there was no one else in the room with her. She had the odd feeling that she and her family were in danger, and that whoever had yelled at her was trying to warn her. She rushed down to the second floor and checked on her children. She was relieved to find they were all safe and sound, sleeping peacefully in their rooms. She went down to the main floor and found, much to her surprise, a lit candle lying on its side on a wooden windowsill. She believes it was lit and tipped over shortly before she arrived. Had she not been startled and gone to check, Niki and her family might have been trapped in a burning building. Niki didn't know who she had to thank for disturbing her, and more concerning than that, she didn't know who to blame for trying to burn down her restaurant and home. Another thing she didn't know at the time was that the entire town of Port Perry had a history of fire.

A fire began in a Port Perry hotel in November of 1883 and spread rapidly through the town's wooden buildings. The fire consumed everything in its path and burned much of the downtown. Not much could be repaired right away due to the winter weather. Then tragedy struck again in July of 1884 when another fire began in a different hotel. Only two downtown buildings that housed businesses weren't reduced to ashes that time: a general store and a hotel that was originally on the site of the restaurant. And then, a short while later, a third fire broke out in a confectionary store that adjoined the hotel. The fire brigade was quick to respond and put out the fire before it spread too far, but the hotel was burned to the ground. No newspaper accounts of this fire exist; yet another fire in the newspaper office had destroyed years of records.

Given the town's history, it's not too surprising that one of the restaurant's ghosts is trying to protect it from fire. If only all the spirits had the best interests of the building and its owners at heart. Most seem dead set on tormenting the living.

Niki often spotted an old woman watching her as she worked, and the television regularly turned off while Niki was watching it. One night Niki tried to leave her bedroom, only to find the door impossible to budge. She called a friend to come to her rescue. When her friend arrived, the door opened from the outside without a hitch.

One of Niki's staff members once called her in the middle of the night, terrified. He didn't want to be left alone in the building ever again. After the last diner had left the restaurant that night, the staff member had locked the door and turned out all the lights. He turned around and saw an old woman serving a young couple seated at table thirteen. A flickering candle illuminated their pale faces. The man quit soon thereafter.

Soon the day came for Niki to move on too. She sold the business in 1997 to Sam Chiusolo, his son, Scott, and his daughter, Joanne, but the sale got off to a rocky start. During a meeting in the dining room to discuss the sale, a decorative plate displayed on a wall-mounted shelf flew into the air and split into three pieces. Two of those pieces shattered on the floor, but the third struck Sam on the head. Despite this ominous sign, the Chiusolo family proceeded with the purchase.

Scott had to deal with the ghosts' antics on a near daily basis. He was often the first to arrive at work, only to find that the front door had been bolted from the inside, and he regularly heard footsteps going down the staircase when he was the last person remaining in the building.

Guests and staff frequently had hair-raising experiences in the women's washroom — from watching the stall doors close and lock on their own to seeing a woman enter and disappear before their eyes. One day Joanne was cleaning the bathroom when one of the stall doors opened and closed three times in rapid succession.

Joanne had never been physically attacked by the ghosts, but Sam hadn't been so lucky. Not only did the piece of china strike his head, but he was once pushed from behind while he was doing some routine maintenance in the basement. Another night, while on his way home, he realized he had forgotten some important papers. He returned to the restaurant and opened the front door, but as soon as he stepped into the building a pair of invisible arms grabbed him from behind and wrapped him in a tight bear hug that lasted for nearly fifteen seconds. Ice-cold chills spread through Sam's entire body and the experience left him shaken, both physically and mentally. In 1998 the Chiusolo family sold the restaurant, which was eventually renamed Jester's Court.

The dining area of Jester's Court

Plenty of kitchen and serving staff have witnessed odd phenomena over the years, such as banging on the doors and walls, the sound of someone whistling in an otherwise empty room, lights and electronics turning on and off and personal belongings mysteriously going missing. But Debbie Burton has witnessed far more than her fair share.

She'd heard rumours around town that the restaurant was haunted but she'd never given them any serious consideration. Not until she was hired as a server in 1997. One night, after working a late shift, Debbie stepped outside onto the front porch. Nearly as soon as she closed the door, she heard the bolt lock from the inside.

"Oh, fine," she said, throwing her hands in the air. "Lock me out. I'm finished for the day anyway!"

It was the first time she had had to deal with one of the ghosts, but it was far from the last.

One night Debbie walked the last customers out of the restaurant, locked the front door, and made her way back to the dining area to finish her closing duties. But the interior door to the main dining area wouldn't open. In fact, Debbie couldn't even turn the doorknob. It was as if someone was holding it tightly on the other side.

"Let me in!" Debbie shouted. "Stop playing this game! I have to close up!"

The doorknob suddenly twisted and the door swung open. There was no one on the other side.

Another night she walked from the first floor to the second turning off all the lights, but when she returned to the main floor all of the lights had been turned back on.

In her typical fashion, Debbie addressed the spirits

directly. "If you want the lights on I'll leave them on."

Debbie has had at least two notable experiences with the ghosts while working with Karen, one of the cooks. They were clearing up dishes following another busy night when, out of the corner of her eye, Karen saw a shadow pass by. She turned and saw a woman wearing a long navy blue dress approaching her — but as soon as the stranger reached the centre of the room, she disappeared. Debbie wasn't surprised by what Karen had seen, as earlier in the evening she herself had heard two ghosts giggling in the empty kitchen.

Another night one of the ghosts, perhaps the lady in the blue dress, turned on the fans above the gas stoves right after Karen had turned them off.

"Shut them off!" Debbie shouted.

The fans shut off. Neither Debbie nor Karen was particularly surprised; they'd grown accustomed to the ghosts' antics. But they were irritated when, a short while later, the fans turned on again. They entered the kitchen prepared to yell at the ghosts but were shocked to discover the kitchen fryers had been turned on too. The ghosts had crossed a line from annoying to dangerous.

"When you play with fire, you get burned," Debbie said, in her sternest voice. "You could burn this place down, so you had better stop it now."

Given the town's history, it's peculiar — or perhaps it isn't — that the ghosts often do things that could easily start another fire. It's also peculiar that anyone who has spent some time listening to a handful of Debbie's tales would doubt Jester's Court is haunted, but one of her friends used to be a staunch skeptic. He and Debbie, along with a few other friends, were having lunch together beside the main-floor fireplace when the talk naturally turned to the ghosts. After Debbie had shared some of her most compelling accounts, there was a brief lull in the conversation.

"I still don't believe that ghosts exist in this place," the skeptic proclaimed loudly, filling the silence.

Without warning, the salt shaker flew off the table and landed right in front of him, and then a number of framed pictures on the wall turned sideways.

"Look at that!" Debbie said loudly, pointing to the pictures as proof her friend was wrong.

The pictures slowly rotated back to their original position as the group sat and stared at them in shock, their eyes wide and their mouths hanging open. The man who hadn't believed in ghosts had become a believer, joining the throngs of people who have had dealings with the paranormal in Jester's Court.

BEYOND THE VEIL

Saint John, New Brunswick

On a whim Doreen Damon decided to visit her mother. It had been a while since she'd seen her, so she called a taxi and told the driver where she wanted to go. But as she drove along her mother's street, Doreen got the feeling that something was terribly wrong.

The window coverings in all of the neighbours' houses were drawn tight. It was an old English custom that meant someone had died.

Doreen rushed out of the taxi to her mother's door. It opened before she could knock. Someone Doreen thought she knew was standing inside.

"You're too late, Doreen," the person said. "She's dead."

"No, she's not!" Doreen shouted. There was no way. It wasn't possible. Her mother couldn't be dead; she *couldn't* .

But then Doreen saw the coffin.

Doreen still couldn't bring herself to accept that her mother had died. She ran to the coffin, looked inside, saw her mother's body laid out, and then did something no one could have expected — not even Doreen herself. She reached in and hugged her mother's lifeless body tight.

Her mother's eyes suddenly flew open.

Doreen woke up with a start. Her heart was pounding and she was drenched in a cold sweat. It took her a while to realize she'd been dreaming. Her mother was still alive. And Doreen hadn't travelled home to visit her mother in England; she was still in Lakewood Heights, a neighbourhood of Saint John where she lived with her husband, Hazen, and their children. Doreen was relieved, but it took some time to fall back asleep.

Not too long after that disturbing nightmare, Doreen's family in England called with some sad news. Her mother's health was failing. She'd been diagnosed with cancer and didn't have much time to live. Doreen was devastated. She'd had no idea. Not only did they live far apart, but her mother had never been one to complain, so she hadn't mentioned the cancer to Doreen.

Doreen got on a plane to England as soon as she could. She spent as much time with her mother as possible before returning home to her family and her job.

Shortly after returning to Canada, her family called again, this time to let Doreen know her mother had died. But, they said, she'd been content that she'd been able to see her daughter one final time.

A few days later, still deep in grief, Doreen took a nap

on her couch. She woke up suddenly — someone had placed a hand on hers for a moment before moving on.

Doreen sat up with a start and saw who'd touched her. It was her mother, gliding up the stairs and disappearing from sight. Doreen broke down and cried.

Although this wasn't common for Doreen, she wasn't surprised that she'd had a prophetic dream or that she'd been visited by her mother's ghost. She'd been born with a caul, what her mother had called a veil. It's a rare occurrence in which a baby is born with a piece of the amniotic sac attached to their head or face. It's harmless and removed immediately. But due to its rarity, there is a great deal of superstition around it. Many people believe a caul is a sign that a baby has second sight, the ability to predict the future. Keeping the removed caul is said to bring good luck. Accordingly, Doreen's mother kept the caul and, when Doreen was older, advised her to "give up every cent you have but don't ever give up your veil."

So Doreen never did. She kept the caul even when she moved to Saint John. She and Hazen owned and operated a number of supermarkets around the city. When they opened a store in the neighbourhood of Chipman Hill in the 1970s, Doreen had another paranormal encounter.

She and Hazen had searched for a home close to the supermarket for a long time without success and were forced to sleep in the store. Finally they heard about a house in a perfect location. The old woman who lived there had recently died, and her daughter lived with her husband in Toronto. The daughter agreed to rent the house to the Damons, and Doreen, Hazen and their children promptly moved in. Although the house was a little dreary, Doreen and Hazen were relieved they didn't need to spend one more night in their store. But their son Allen wasn't happy.

He didn't like the house, not one bit. Although he was old enough to stay home alone, he hated being the only one there. Even during the day when it was beautiful and sunny outside, Allen preferred to hang out in the store with his parents rather than remain in that house alone, because he never felt truly alone — not in the dead woman's house.

The family had moved in during the winter, so come spring Doreen was eager to plant some flowers in the front yard. She grabbed her trowel and some bulbs and headed outside. She had crouched down to dig a hole when all of a sudden she heard a loud racket of bony knuckles rapping on the front window. She spun around in shock, but there wasn't a soul to be seen. Hazen was at work, the children were at school and Doreen was alone. Thanks to her second sight, Doreen was certain the rapping had been the ghost of the old woman and that she didn't want Doreen to plant her bulbs where she'd planned. And with that, Doreen scrapped her gardening.

She was hardly surprised when a beautiful bunch of flowers bloomed in the exact spot she had nearly dug up. Had she done so, she likely would have ruined the previously planted bulbs, and that was clearly something the resident ghost couldn't tolerate. The old woman was fortunate to have someone who had been born with a veil — someone with second sight — move into her house.

THE BICKLEIGH GHOST

Bickleigh, Saskatchewan

Ivy and Annie Bristow were in good spirits. The sisters had spent the evening at their neighbour's house and were enjoying a peaceful sleigh ride home. It was a cold night in 1932, but they were warm under thick blankets, and the moon gave the countryside a beautiful, almost ethereal glow. As they approached the railway tracks, their horses stopped suddenly, nearly throwing the sisters from the sleigh. The animals snorted loudly, stomped their hooves in the snow, and refused to move any farther. Clearly something had spooked them.

Ivy and Annie nervously cast aside their blankets and stood up in the sleigh to see what had startled their horses. Neither sister could believe the sight that met their eyes. There was another rider approaching them quickly, but both the man and the horse appeared to be made of mist and light, not flesh and bone. Not only that, the horse was bearing down on them nearly as quickly as a locomotive but without making a sound.

As soon as the spectral rider had passed, the sisters' horses bolted and sped all the way back to the Bristow farm without slowing down. Ivy and Annie kept their eyes on the road behind them as they travelled, too afraid that whatever had passed might decide to turn around and come back for them. It's the earliest known sighting of the Bickleigh Ghost, a spectre that has haunted the entire town ever since that night.

The next year Joe Pitzel, a schoolteacher, and Joe Ellis, Pitzel's roommate, had their own unsettling encounter with the Bickleigh Ghost. The men had just extinguished the coal oil lamp that stood on a nightstand between their beds in the boarding house bedroom they shared, plunging the room into darkness.

Ping! Ping! Clang!

It was the sound of a few coins falling from the nightstand and hitting the floor. The coins were heard rolling across the room and slowly spinning to a stop.

Bang!

Clatter!

A pocket knife had fallen after the coins, followed by a pen.

"Do you hear that?" Pitzel asked.

"I sure do!" Ellis replied.

They leapt from their beds and lit a match. The light danced in a jerky fashion around the room thanks to the trembling hand that held the match, and the men were quick to see what had happened. A cloth that normally lay smooth on the nightstand to protect its surface was pulled forward. And the lamp that sat at the back of the nightstand, against the wall, was hanging perilously over the front edge of the table.

The men returned the lamp to its regular position and lit it so they could properly examine the room. The door and window were locked and there was no one hiding anywhere. Neither Pitzel nor Ellis could explain who — or what — had thrown their items to the floor.

It wasn't the last time the Bickleigh Ghost terrorized Joe Pitzel. A little while after the nightstand incident — enough time to begin sleeping through the night again but not nearly enough to have forgotten what had happened — Joe was enjoying an early evening dinner with his good friend Mac McLean, who was a United Grain Growers agent and worked in the Bickleigh grain elevator. Joe and Mac had just begun eating in the elevator's living quarters when they heard heavy footsteps pass through the nearby office, march down the stairs leading to the living quarters, and stop on the other side of the door.

The men watched the door and waited for it to open. It didn't.

"Come on in," Mac yelled, through a mouthful of half-chewed food, assuming a friend or co-worker was waiting outside to be invited in.

No one answered, and still the door remained closed.

"Come on in!" Mac repeated, this time much louder as he grew a little frustrated.

Silence and stillness answered.

"Someone's trying to scare us," Joe said, as he stood up and crossed the room. "Let's find out who it is."

He opened the door. No one was there. They split up and quickly searched the entire property, from the office to the engine room to the silo. They found no one, only farming equipment and grain. Joe knew beyond a shadow of a doubt that he'd once again been in the presence of the dead.

George Redhead, a farmer who had bought a plot of land through which the Canadian Pacific Railway ran, had never heard of the Bickleigh Ghost. Not that the knowledge would have likely swayed his decision to purchase the property. He was a hard-working man who toiled from dawn to dusk, breaking soil, chopping through thick roots and digging up large rocks as he prepared his land to be farmed. Not having built his house yet, he slept outside on the ground, and then, when the sun rose the next morning, he'd get up and commence the day's work. Until, that is, one night when George had an experience eerily similar to that of the Bristow sisters, except with one key difference.

He'd just gotten comfortable when he heard horse hooves charging through the woods straight for him. Alarmed that he might be trampled in his makeshift shelter, George scurried out into the open, where he could be seen. His fear quickly turned to confusion, then back to fear. The sound of hooves carried right past him, no more than a metre or two away, and then faded into the distance — but George had seen neither man nor animal.

Sometime later two men snuck into an abandoned house on the outskirts of town, about five kilometres beyond George's land. They were hunting for antiques or anything of value they could steal, and their search led them down into the cellar. The air smelled musty and it was so dark they could barely see their own hands in front of their faces. They hadn't found anything worth taking when the front door opened. Had it been the wind? An animal? Either of those explanations would have been far, far more reassuring than the truth.

After a brief, silent pause during which the men heard nothing but their own rapidly beating hearts, footsteps walked across the floor overhead. Summoning as much courage as they could muster, the men crept up the cellar steps and peeked out of the doorway. They didn't see anyone where they'd heard the footsteps stop. The abandoned house seemed to be as empty as it had been when they'd first snuck inside. They searched the rest of the house but still didn't find anyone, so they ran outside thinking whoever had entered must have exited. Although the house was in an open field with nowhere to hide for two or three kilometres in every direction, there wasn't a soul to be seen. Far too scared to re-enter the house they now believed to be haunted, the men gave up their search and quickly fled the property, running all the way back to town.

By 1980 the section of railway that ran through Bickleigh was abandoned. Within a year the rails and ties were taken up; some were reused elsewhere and the rest of the scrap was sold. The timing seems portentous, as shortly thereafter, in 1982, a farmer made a gruesome discovery that appears to tie everything together and shed light on the Bickleigh Ghost.

Bickleigh, Saskatchewan, 1956

Bruce McDonald was working in his field less than one kilometre from the former location of the tracks when he saw an odd round white rock protruding from the dirt. He yanked it free from the earth and prepared to throw it aside, then froze. He wasn't holding a rock. He was holding a human skull.

Buried in the same location were an arm bone, a rib and a leg bone. The Department of Anthropology at the University of Saskatchewan studied the human remains and determined the bones had belonged to a twenty-five-year-old male who had died approximately sixty years before. These findings got the locals talking. Not just because of the macabre nature of the discovery, but also because of a story the oldest among them used to tell back in the day — a story that had not been shared for some time. But now, of course, was the perfect time to drag that old, dusty story out of the shadows and share it once again.

In 1924, eight years before the Bristow sisters first saw the Bickleigh Ghost and fifty-eight years before the skull was discovered in Bruce's field, the railway was being extended from the town of Milden to McMorran. It was back-breaking work performed in some of the harshest conditions, and by the time the line reached Bickleigh, winter had arrived. Horses that had literally been worked to death were buried in shallow graves, and the combination of stress and exhaustion caused tempers to flare and many fights to break out among the men.

Late one night the most heated fight yet erupted between two men. When the sun rose the next morning and the crew dragged themselves back to work, one of the two men who'd been in the fight had mysteriously disappeared. Many suspected foul play, and one person wanted to search the surrounding area for a freshly covered grave not occupied by a dead horse, but no one had the energy to do so. Plus, the job was so gruelling that men regularly quit and walked away without so much as a farewell. Life went on and the missing man — who'd been twenty-five the last time he was seen alive — was more or less forgotten.

Until 1982. The locals connected the dots and grew convinced the man had indeed been murdered, and that his spirit — along with one of the horses that had died in Bickleigh — was responsible for all of the ghost sightings that had plagued the town over the years.

These days there's not much left of Bickleigh. Although it was once a thriving town with a school, post office and general store in addition to two grain elevators, it's now a very small farming community. Most of the residents have either moved on or passed away, but there's one man who can neither move on nor die. Well, he can't die *again*. And so the Bickleigh Ghost continues to ride through the night and walk through empty houses, striking fear into all who hear and see him.

THE GHOST iN THE GLASS

Creston, British Columbia

Frederick William Lindsay, known as Fred to most, was living the high life. He was young, single and didn't have a care in the world. Throughout the 1920s he'd drifted around British Columbia following his passions, working odd jobs when he needed money and spending his earnings without hesitation. And then, in 1929, the Great Depression began and Fred's life changed drastically.

Work was hard to come by. Fred could no longer afford to live a carefree life. Like many people living during the worst economic downturn of the industrialized age, he could barely afford to eat. But soon Fred heard of a project that could kick-start the local economy in the Kootenay region: construction of the Goat River Dam, which would provide electricity to the nearby town of Creston. After a long journey to a remote part of the province, Fred signed up for the gruelling work project that only paid seven dollars per month. It was a big change from his previous way of life, but it was better than starving.

But old habits die hard, and Fred continued to spend all of his meagre earnings no sooner than the coins had settled in his pocket. So he was too broke one evening in November of 1932 to join his workmates at a local dance. He found himself sitting alone in the dark, empty bunkhouse, bored out of his wits and trying to think of a way to pass the time. And then the perfect idea struck him. Someone had once told him during his travels that, under the right circumstances, a simple glass of water could be used to communicate with spirits. With nothing to lose, he filled a glass with water and set it on the table before him.

Fred stared at the water, the eerie glow of his coal lamp casting long, thin shadows across the cold room. In the emptiness of the bunkhouse, every sound was amplified; the wind outside shrieked, the walls groaned and Fred could hear the beating of his own heart. But nothing happened. The water remained free and clear of visions. Fred began to feel silly. What if his friends returned early and saw him? What would they think? What would he say? Telling them the truth would make him sound like he'd lost his mind. If nothing else, he was sure the teasing would be long-lasting and fierce. He decided to abandon the foolish experiment and dump the glass of water.

But before he moved, something happened. The clear water turned cloudy and swirled around the glass until it was milky white. Fred couldn't believe his eyes. A small black patch blossomed in the centre of the white liquid like something rotten, like a disease. The black patch slowly took on the shape of a face, a face that was staring intently at Fred. It was a man wearing a hooded robe, a man with anger in his eyes. Fred felt like he'd made a mistake, but it was too late. The spirit he'd summoned was already there, and he didn't appear to be friendly.

From within the glass, the man shook his fists at Fred and yelled at him, although Fred couldn't hear what he was saying. As he stared in disbelief at his homemade crystal ball, Fred suddenly recognized the ghost in the glass. It was an old friend of his, Jack "Black Jack" McFarlane, who had recently died. Moments after Fred made this realization, Jack disappeared, the cloudiness swirled out of existence, and the glass of water returned to normal. But Fred's fear — and a flurry of questions — remained. Why had Jack's ghost visited him? Why had he been so angry? Fearing he'd opened a door between the worlds of the living and the dead, he quickly dumped the water and went to bed, hoping to put the entire experience behind him.

Time passed and with every day Fred began to forget about the whole thing. Life returned to its normal routine of long hours of hard work and little respite. Until one day during the last week of January 1933, when a trapper stayed with the workers in the bunkhouse for a few nights. The newcomer was blessed with the gift of gab and entertained everyone — especially Fred — with tales of his travels. One particular tidbit of information caught Fred's attention: there was a miner living and working on the Monashee Mountains who was looking for a partner.

That sounded like music to Fred's ears. The other workers tried to talk Fred out of joining the mysterious miner — cautioning him that he shouldn't risk the security of his job on what sounded like a wild goose chase, a wintery search that could very well claim his life — but Fred had already made up his mind. On February 2 he gathered all the food and supplies he could buy or borrow, including a pair of battered snowshoes, and set out into the wild alone. The snow was deep and the air was frigid, and by ten o'clock that night, Fred was exhausted. Doubt began to seep into his mind. What if he never found the miner? What if the miner didn't actually exist? The only thing that kept him from turning around was the teasing his old workmates would give him if he returned so soon.

But around midnight things got worse. The temperature suddenly warmed up and the snow turned to rain. Within minutes Fred was soaking wet from head to toe. He wanted to stop and rest but he knew if he did that, if he allowed himself to fall asleep, he probably wouldn't wake up. He forced his legs to keep moving and pushed on as hypothermia began to set in. He didn't make it far.

The rain turned back to snow as the temperature plummeted. A strong wind blew in from the north, freezing Fred's water-soaked clothing. He tried to keep walking but fell to his knees. The mountains were in sight, but it didn't matter; Fred had nothing left in the tank. He should have listened to his friends when they'd tried to talk him out of leaving. He should have turned back when he'd first feared he might be in danger. Instead, all he could do was drag himself to the base of a large tree and prepare for death.

But then something caught his eye. A black shape appeared in the middle of the swirling white snow, about fifteen metres in the distance. It was a man in a black hood, gesturing for Fred to follow. It took Fred a moment to realize why he felt like he was experiencing déjà vu. The hooded man was Black Jack, and Fred had seen this exact vision before, back on the night he'd stared into his glass of water. Now Fred realized why Jack's spirit had appeared to be so angry: he was upset to have been forced out of his eternal rest in order to save his living friend from freezing to death in a snowstorm.

Only one of the two men left footprints in the snow as Jack led Fred through the storm. It looked to Fred as if his old friend was gliding a few centimetres above the ground. Soon they passed down a slope and Fred couldn't believe his eyes. There was a small cabin not too far away, so close to where he thought he would die. He turned to thank his phantom friend, but Jack had disappeared.

The door was unlocked and there was a small bed covered in warm blankets in the corner. Fred collapsed to the bed, wrapped the blankets tight around his body, and slept for the better part of a day. When he woke up, he found some food on the shelves in the cabin. After eating he began to feel like a new man, and when he stepped outside, he found that the storm had stopped and it wasn't nearly as cold as it had been the night before.

Although Fred never saw Jack again, it was as if his old friend was guiding him from regions beyond, for Fred lucked upon the miner he'd set out to meet and even became his partner. And he owed it all to a glass of water.

A CHRISTMAS POLTERGEIST

Eastern Passage, Nova Scotia

It was Christmas Eve 1943, but Eastern Passage, a quiet suburb of Dartmouth, was uncharacteristically dark. None of the houses or the trees that lined the streets were lit with the typical strings of colourful Christmas lights. World War II was being fought overseas, and Canadians at home were trying to conserve energy to meet the needs of wartime industry. But for the Hilchie family, in their modest home that bordered the woodland near the Shearwater Air Force Station, the night was about to light up. Not with twinkling lights, but with blind terror.

Louis, Ethel and their five children were preparing for bed when a face appeared outside one of their windows. The curly-haired stranger stared inside at the family with an unseasonably angry expression, and his face seemed to float in the air as if it had no body below it at all. The Hilchies — particularly the children — were immediately afraid of the man, and a search of the property that turned up no sign of the stranger did not to quell their fears.

Although the man wasn't seen again that night, he certainly made his presence known.

Bang! Bang! Bang!

Three loud knocks thundered throughout the house, reverberating through the walls. They had seemed to come from all over the place and didn't sound like they had been produced by a human fist — instead, they had an odd, hollow sound that scared the family more than before. The banging continued sporadically throughout the night, and Ethel felt it shaking the furniture, floorboards and hand-rail as she made her weary way to bed.

That night two of the younger children asked to sleep in Ethel's bed. She agreed without hesitation. But none of them had a peaceful sleep, for not long after they'd turned out the light, something yanked the blanket and sheets clean off the bed. Ethel quickly covered her children again and, thinking one of them might have kicked the sheets off, lay between them, gently pinning each child's legs to the mattress with her own. It didn't work. Once again, as soon as she turned off the light, invisible hands ripped the bedding off. Ethel knew their house was being haunted by a poltergeist.

Poltergeists thrive on making loud noises and throwing objects across rooms in an effort to terrorize the living. The Hilchies' Christmas poltergeist certainly fit that bill. On Christmas Day and throughout the week that followed, the knocking continued at random times without warning. One day the washing machine scooted across the floor in fits and starts as if it had sprouted legs and was learning to walk on its own. Another time Ethel and three of her children couldn't believe their eyes when the table they were sitting around suddenly flipped over with a terrible crash. Not too long after that, one of the daughters, Catherine, watched in horror as invisible hands picked up an egg and cracked it into the frying pan heating on the stove. If the ghost was trying to be helpful, Catherine didn't appreciate the gesture.

Desperate to rid their home of the poltergeist and not knowing where else to turn, Mr. and Mrs. Hilchie called both the local police and staff at the *Mail-Star*, a local newspaper, shortly after New Year's Day. They couldn't take it anymore. Corporal Harold Johnson of the Dartmouth Royal Canadian Mounted Police detachment was assigned the case. He observed some of the paranormal activity himself, such as one of the young Hilchie daughters, Rita, receiving prophetic messages through a Ouija board. He could find no logical explanation for the terrifying events that were taking place in the house and therefore could offer the family no assistance.

Meanwhile, the journalists who visited the house had no shortage of eerie events to write about, and soon articles about the family and their poltergeist began to fill the newspaper's pages. A pair of scissors sitting on a shelf slid across the wood, opening and closing as if trying to slice through the air. A pot of boiling water meant for tea flew off the stove and crashed to the floor. A bowl of hot soup levitated off the kitchen table and dumped its contents in poor Catherine's lap. A rocking chair slid across the room as if being pulled by an invisible rope, with one of the daughters sitting as still as a statue on it, too terrified to move a muscle. The lights turned on and off on their own. An alarm clock sailed off a dresser. Pillows, boxes of soap and a tub of shortening were thrown down the stairs.

The sensational reports spread far and wide, and soon curious thrill-seekers were travelling great distances to see the Hilchies' haunted house for themselves. So many people made the trek that the R.C.M.P. had to return in order to direct traffic. The congestion might have annoyed the Hilchies' neighbours, but that would have been at the bottom of the family's concerns, for the poltergeist's activities were beginning to turn from frightening to life-threatening.

One of the journalists was struck by a flying pillow. He was lucky; the ghost soon began throwing hammers. And twice Ethel was tripped on the stairs, causing her to fall to the bottom. The first time she was fortunate and avoided injury. The second time she did not; the heel of her left shoe was yanked backwards, and the fall resulted in a broken ankle and wrenched shoulder.

All of the newspaper coverage caught the attention of Dr. Thomas L. Garrett, president and founder of the Garrett Foundation for Psychological Research. That spring the doctor travelled from his home in New York to interview the Hilchies and investigate their case. Dr. Garrett had been responsible for debunking many claims of paranormal activity over the years, but if he thought he'd find a hoax during his trip to Eastern Passage, he had another think coming. Shortly after he began talking with the Hilchies in their kitchen, a teapot flew off its hook, sailed across the room, and nearly struck the eldest daughter, Gladys, on the head.

Dr. Garrett concluded that the Hilchies were indeed dealing with a poltergeist, and that the activity seemed to be centred around Catherine. After hearing this, Catherine admitted she'd once again seen the curly-haired man through a window the day before — the same stranger whose Christmas Eve appearance had seemingly set off the string of events. Dr. Garrett later wrote that the Hilchie case was one of the most unusual in all his years of experience.

Louis and Ethel had been tormented enough. That spring they tore down the house and built a new one a few metres away. The poltergeist didn't return. But their memories couldn't be rebuilt; those they had to live with for the rest of their days.

NEVER LET GO OF THE PAST

Ottawa, Ontario

They talked about feeling uneasy when alone in the restaurant late at night. They talked about sensing an unseen presence in the old stone building. They talked about disembodied footsteps, flickering lights and electrical equipment turning on by itself. Worst of all, they talked about a spirit lingering within the walls, a spirit that hated the living, a spirit that wanted everyone alive to *get out*!

But that's all a young woman who'd recently been hired as a server in the Courtyard Restaurant thought it was: just talk. Her new co-workers were trying to scare her. That was all. It was clearly nothing more than an initiation ritual, a practical joke played on new employees. Even if one or two of the staff members believed they'd heard or seen something unusual, they probably had overactive imaginations. That's all.

Well, she wouldn't let them scare her. She didn't believe in ghosts. And if the stories scared other staff members from working late, all the better. She welcomed the extra income she earned thanks to all of the extra late-night shifts she picked up. Few people wanted to stay past closing, even employees who'd worked there for many, many years, which she had to admit was a little odd. If the stories were simply meant to scare new staff, why were the veterans afraid? The young woman didn't give it too much thought — better not to look a gift horse in the mouth. She was happy to work as late as her manager asked. For a while, anyway.

But then, after a few months, something unusual happened. She was alone on the second floor, closing the restaurant. It was dark. And cold. And quiet.

And then it wasn't. Footsteps cut through the silence in the hallway, coming toward her. Hesitantly, she poked her head through the doorway, into the hall. There was no one there. But the footsteps continued to come closer, and closer, and closer . . .

Suddenly someone brushed against her. Shivers shot up her spine. Goosebumps spread across her skin. The footsteps carried on past her, down the hall, and slowly faded in the distance.

The young woman turned in the opposite direction, walked downstairs to the kitchen, picked up the largest, sharpest knife she could find, and sat down on the floor in the middle of the room with the knife in front of her —

ready to strike anything that came near. Then she called her boyfriend to come pick her up and sat as still as a statue until he arrived. She no longer doubted the stories. It hadn't just been talk. The Courtyard Restaurant was haunted.

Located in the heart of downtown Ottawa's ByWard Market, a lively area filled with trendy stores and popular bars and restaurants, the Courtyard Restaurant at 21 George Street has a long and tragic history. Originally built in 1827 as a log tavern, its wood walls were eventually replaced with limestone, and bedrooms were added to welcome overnight guests. In 1866 the building was leased to the federal government and served as a military garrison. For six years up to 150 soldiers were stationed there, and the courtyard in front of the building, which would eventually give the present-day restaurant its name, was the site of many military hangings. More than forty years later, many more people would die on the premises when the building was used as a civil emergency centre during the typhoid epidemic of 1911 and 1912. But most people believe the ghost that haunts its halls dates back to a fire that destroyed much of the block on July 29, 1872.

Although a number of people were initially trapped in the building, all managed to escape the flames. However, one of the hotel guests, a woman named Mrs. Evans, rushed back into the burning building to retrieve some papers she'd left in her room on the second floor. It was a terrible decision that cost Mrs. Evans her life. The survivors who had made it out stood and watched helplessly as the flames consumed the building and smoke billowed through the collapsed roof. Mrs. Evans' wild and pain-stricken howls filled the night, an awful sound that sickened everyone in the courtyard.

Those who see her ghost agree that Mrs. Evans not only wants to be left alone, but that her presence gives off a hostile energy. Why she appears to be angry at the living is unclear. Perhaps she's jealous of those who live and breathe. Perhaps she doesn't realize she's dead and has no idea why people continue to invade her personal space. Or perhaps she simply never cared too much for people, even before she met her unfortunate end. But whatever the case, her presence regularly causes people to panic, like the young woman who found comfort by holding a kitchen knife while she waited for her boyfriend to arrive. Other staff members have forgotten personal items on the second floor and refused to go back for them, opting instead to retrieve them the next day when it was nice and bright outside, and much less spooky inside.

People who have seen Mrs. Evans in the flesh, so to speak, have described her as having a stern look. She wears a long black Victorian dress. She likes to make glasses chime and slide salt and pepper shakers across tables. Her presence is usually preceded by a sudden, extreme drop in temperature. And she is most often seen staring out at the street from one of the second floor dining room windows. A manager once caught sight of Mrs. Evans staring through the window late one night after everyone else had left. The manager assumed the woman was a customer who had lingered in the restaurant — she scanned the rest of the floor, but when she turned back to Mrs. Evans, she discovered she'd disappeared.

Cynthia Verboven had a few run-ins with Mrs. Evans herself when she was the Courtyard's senior event coordinator. The ghost once ripped a whiteboard off the wall and tossed it across Cynthia's office in the middle of a meeting, causing it to land with a loud bang on her desk. Another time, Cynthia had finished setting up the dining room according to a guest's specifications and left the room. When she returned, Cynthia discovered that Mrs. Evans had moved a high chair away from the fireplace. It was an uncharacteristically thoughtful move on Mrs. Evans' part, but also an understandable one given the tragic circumstances of her own death.

In 2019 a mysterious fog hovering near the bar was captured by one of the restaurant's interior security cameras. When Cynthia enlarged the image, she couldn't believe her eyes . . . nor the eyes staring back at her from the photo. Clearly visible within the fog was the face of a woman — Mrs. Evans. Could the fog have been part of her ghostly form, or perhaps traces of the smoke that claimed her life so many years ago?

It would be bad enough if Mrs. Evans' appearances were limited to within the Courtyard Restaurant, but at least once she has also appeared outside. Not on the ground, mind you, but hovering two storeys up in the air. A woman named Lidia, who used to live in the neighbourhood, was standing in the middle of the courtyard one summer evening in the mid-1990s. She was chatting with a friend when she happened to look up and caught sight of Mrs. Evans, dressed in her distinctive black gown, staring down at her from above. At first Lidia thought the woman must be a statue affixed to the wall, since she hadn't moved a muscle. But then Mrs. Evans suddenly glided a metre or two to her side, looked directly at Lidia with anger in her eyes, and vanished.

Her appearance lasted only a few seconds, and although Lidia had pointed at the spot where the ghost had been, her friend had seen nothing. More than twenty years later, Lidia is still researching the location and its tragic history, hoping to uncover more details about Mrs. Evans and the fire that once consumed the block where the Courtyard Restaurant serves up fine food and dark frights.

Some people — both living and dead — can never let go of the past.

THE GHOST OF FAN TAN ALLEY

Victoria, British Columbia

Charlene White was running late. She'd been shopping in Chinatown with a friend when she realized they'd lost track of time. So they decided to take a shortcut and pass through Fan Tan Alley. It was a decision they'd soon regret.

The night was dark and cool. Other than Charlene and her friend, the alley was practically deserted. But then someone pushed Charlene hard into one of the brick walls and ran past her. Charlene was hurt, scared and more than a little angry.

"Hey!" she shouted. "Watch it!"

The young man — he looked like a teenager — ran out of sight without slowing or stopping to apologize.

"That kid nearly knocked me over," Charlene told her friend.

"What kid?" her friend asked, confused. She'd been walking slightly ahead of Charlene and hadn't seen the collision.

"That kid." Charlene pointed at the far end of the alley. "The kid who just ran by."

Her friend looked from one end of the alley to the other with a frown on her face. "There's no one there." She didn't see a soul.

"I just saw him," Charlene said, a note of uncertainty settling into her voice. *Had* she seen someone? She could have sworn she had, but her friend had been with her the entire time and the alley was so small that it would have been impossible for her to miss anyone else passing by. Maybe no one had run through. But if that was so, who had shoved Charlene into the wall?

On another cold, dark night, a different woman had a nearly identical experience, but this time more than one person saw the teenaged boy run through the alley. Stacy Keller was walking through Fan Tan Alley with her friend when something suddenly broke the silence: footsteps pounding the pavement behind them, approaching fast. Stacy and her friend had just turned to look for the source of the commotion as a young man ran between them and shoved them both against opposite walls. The women turned back around and were shocked to discover he'd disappeared. Terrified, they ran back out in the direction they'd entered the alley only moments before.

Fan Tan Alley is easy to miss unless you know where to look for it, between a small café and a gift shop on the south side of Fisgard Street in Canada's oldest Chinatown.

At its narrowest point — a gap of 1.2 metres — a child could touch both walls at the same time. Running the length of only one block, the alley has more than a dozen independent stores packed together tightly. It's clean and safe these days, but that wasn't always the case.

Fan Tan Alley

The alley is named after the game of Fan Tan because of the gambling dens that long ago called it home. And drug use and other illicit activities used to be commonplace following the Fraser River Gold Rush of 1858. The story that accompanies the ghost of Fan Tan Alley, the young man who has shoved Charlene, Stacy and countless others over the years, is equally sordid.

In 1889 a seventeen-year-old boy named Chan, who worked at the American Hotel, fell madly in love with a young woman named Yo Gum, who lived near Fan Tan

Alley. However, she didn't return his affection, and when Chan proposed marriage she rejected him bluntly.

Chan plummeted into a deep, dark depression and committed an atrocious crime. Late one night Chan grabbed a large, sharp cleaver and went for a walk. When he saw the woman he loved sitting on a windowsill, he swung the knife at her neck as hard as he could, killing her instantly. Covered in blood and suddenly overcome by panic, Chan ran away and hid in Fan Tan Alley, still clutching the cleaver as if his life depended on it. Two days later he was caught and put in jail to await trial, but he would never see his day in court. Chan took his own life in his cell.

Although he didn't move on after death, Chan didn't remain in the jail either. As night falls on Fan Tan Alley, he replays his mad dash through the narrow space, shoving anyone who stands in his way. For some people, such as Helen Connelly, simply seeing the ghost is far worse than being pushed aside by him.

Helen was one of many people on a ghost walk in 2000 when Chan made an appearance, but she was the only person who was able to see him. As John Adams, a local historian and the founder of Discover the Past Tours, was sharing the horrible history of Fan Tan Alley, Helen heard footsteps swiftly approaching from behind. She turned around and saw Chan running straight at her. His shirt and face were coated in blood and he was swinging a cleaver wildly in the air.

Terrified, she screamed and covered her head to protect herself. But when she didn't feel the anticipated sting of the blade, she hesitantly looked up and was shocked to see Chan was gone without a trace.

"Did you see him?" she asked John. "That man?"

John shook his head. He'd seen nothing unusual.

She couldn't believe it, but no one else in the group had seen or heard Chan either.

"Congratulations," John said. "I think you've just seen the ghost of Fan Tan Alley."

Helen hadn't wanted congratulations, not for seeing such a gruesome sight. But since she'd thought she might be killed only a moment before, she'd take it. She was happy to be alive.

THE SEANCE HOUSE

Winnipeg, Manitoba

It was a cold winter night when twelve respected men and women of the community entered a second-floor bedroom in Dr. Thomas Glendenning Hamilton's personal residence, eager to be part of something both scientific and supernatural. Although they hoped to experience something paranormal, those twelve people didn't yet know that a thirteenth soul would join them as the hour grew late. It was March 10, 1930, and a seance was about to begin.

Moments before, the room had been thoroughly searched and inspected by celebrated lawyer Isaac Pitblado, who had been invited to attend the seance in order to verify that any spirits that might appear — should the group be so fortunate — were not produced by hoax or trickery. Isaac reported there was nothing in the room that could be used to fake an encounter with spirits from beyond. Next, Isaac inspected the men by having them remove their coats, vests, ties and shoes before emptying their pockets. The women were inspected with just as much attention to detail by Florence Creighton. With this task complete, the twelve entered the room at 9:10 p.m. The door was sealed behind them with a padlock to ensure no one could get in or out. Florence and her husband, William, remained in the hall to keep watch at the door.

These precautions might seem extensive for something as simple as an entertaining evening spent trying to contact spirits, but there was more to it than that. Thomas Hamilton was not only a doctor but also a leading researcher of the spiritualism movement, and his goal for the gathering was to capture a picture of a ghost.

Even with so many people packed into the average-sized room, it was unnaturally quiet. Time passed slowly as everyone waited for something — anything — to happen. Dr. Hamilton's Scottish nanny, Elizabeth Poole, closed herself in a cabinet to shut herself off from the others, with the intent of opening a bridge to the paranormal world. She exited the cabinet at 9:33 p.m., and Dr. Hamilton took a picture of her. For the next four minutes, the group sang hymns to entice spirits to join them. Ewan, a man who had attended many of Dr. Hamilton's seances over the years, fell into an agitated state and began shaking and stamping his feet. Then all eyes fell on Mary Marshall, sister-in-law to Elizabeth.

She silenced the room with a sharp, hissing *shh!* Everyone quieted immediately. They knew something was about to begin. Mary was a well-respected medium, a person who can communicate with the dead. Although in Mary's case, she didn't just speak *with* spirits; they often spoke *through* her.

After a tense pause, Mary, her hands on the table before her and her eyes sealed tight, seemed to take on an appearance and demeanour altogether unlike her own. And then she spoke in a deep, gruff voice.

"Good evening. Are you all here all right?" Although the words were coming from Mary's mouth, all those assembled knew they were hearing the voice of Walter, a ghost who had communicated with them during previous seances. He'd proven himself to be a mischievous spirit, and this night was no exception. "What did you have for supper?"

"Don't listen to him!" Ewan shouted. He knew Walter liked to play games, asking questions that seemed innocent in an attempt to gain the trust of the living.

Ignoring Ewan, Walter continued to speak through Mary. "Have you got a man here to watch?"

"Yes, he's here," Dr. Hamilton said gravely, pointing at Isaac.

"Have you got anything in your pocket?" Walter asked of Isaac.

Isaac confirmed his pockets were empty, and added he'd personally searched each of the other men's pockets.

"Then you must be rich," Walter joked.

That set Ewan off. He fell into an odd trance and moaned loudly, hardly pausing long enough to breathe. His arms shook and his legs kicked. It didn't seem to those present that he was aware of his surroundings at all.

The group began to sing. They tried to ignore Walter. The ghost left for a few minutes but then returned at 9:47 p.m.

Mary looked directly at Isaac and smiled.

"I want your friend to enjoy himself," Walter said.

Ewan snapped back to the present like an unconscious man suddenly coming to. "Don't pay any attention to him!"

Walter ignored that. "You didn't introduce me to your friend," he said, as Mary continued to stare at Isaac.

The doctor handled the introduction, saying, "It is Mr. Pitblado."

Mary held out her hand and Isaac shook it as if they were meeting for the first time. In an odd sort of way, they were.

"Shut up," Ewan muttered, a slight directed at Walter.

But Ewan didn't appear to bother Walter one bit. "He says that just to amuse you," he said. "Are your cameras all ready?"

"Yes," Dr. Hamilton said, a thrill of excitement shooting through him like a small electrical current. Finally, this was what he had hoped to achieve through the seance.

But Walter had one last trick up his sleeve.

"Did you bring a man in here?" he asked one of the group, a businessman named W. B. Cooper.

"No," Mr. Cooper said, a little confused.

"Or a woman?"

"No."

"Hammy?" Walter said, turning his attention to Dr. Hamilton and addressing him with a patronizing nickname. "Did you bring a man in here?"

Dr. Hamilton nodded and said, once again, that he had brought Isaac Pitblado as an independent observer.

Mary smirked.

"I am glad you said that," Walter said. "I thought I was going to catch you."

Ewan, still clearly agitated, turned the question around and asked Walter if *he* had brought a man into the seance.

"No," Walter said, without a hint of playfulness. "I brought a woman."

Mary turned to face Isaac — who didn't know what the ghost had meant — and Walter addressed him directly.

"You may think this is very funny, but it isn't," he said, dead serious. "Would you care to put your hands on the medium?"

Something had changed, and Walter was clearly no longer in the mood to play around. Isaac agreed and examined Mary to make sure she didn't move or do anything that could somehow produce a fake apparition. Then Isaac noticed something very odd.

"Walter?" he asked, his voice trembling. "Do I see a whitish light all around the medium?"

There was a halo around Mary like she was glowing. Like Walter — or some other spirit — was beginning to materialize.

"Yes, it is building now," Walter said. "I am placing the form on the chair . . . It is just like a lot of little clouds coming together."

Ewan gasped and wheezed as he struggled to breathe. Elizabeth fell into a deep trance and couldn't be roused.

Dr. Hamilton asked Walter if he had anything else to

tell them, but Ewan didn't allow the ghost to respond.

"Don't bother him!" he shouted. "Don't bother him, for goodness' sake!"

And then the moment of truth finally arrived. Walter used Mary's palm to slam the table as he shouted, "One!"

Slam!

"Two!"

Slam!

"Three!"

Slam!

"Fire!"

Slam!

On the word *fire*, and the fourth slam of Mary's hand, Dr. Hamilton took the picture.

Mary Marshall and W. B. Cooper with a ghost between them, March 10, 1930

When the photograph was developed later that evening, no one could believe what they had captured. Sitting between Mary and Mr. Cooper, on an extra chair that had been empty all night, was a woman no one recognized. Her face stared out from the ectoplasm. Walter had held up his end of the bargain. He had brought another ghost to the seance.

Or had he? Although neither Dr. Hamilton's methods nor his results were questioned during his life, it's challenging to look at the photographs today and not wonder if they might have been a hoax. But the medical association praised his scientific mind at his memorial in 1935, and his wife and children never believed the seances were staged in any way. At the time of the Hamilton experiments, the world at large wanted to believe in seances and the ability to communicate with the dead.

The seance of March 10, 1930 wasn't the last one Dr. Hamilton held in his house, nor was it the last time he captured photographic evidence of paranormal activity. At a time when the high cost of a camera made it rare for a family to own one, he installed no less than a dozen cameras along one wall of the room. And with these cameras, the group took hundreds of photographs, which are now part of the University of Manitoba Archives and Special Collections. The photos show furniture levitating, ectoplasm hanging in the air above people's heads or surrounding the medium's face, and the smoky bodies and faces of spectres peering out of the spirit world . . . directly into ours.

News of Dr. Hamilton's seances first spread across

Canada, then North America and finally the world. People were astounded by his photographs and impressed by the rigorous scientific methods he employed, habits he developed from his medical background. He was regarded as the country's leading expert in the paranormal, a distinction that hasn't diminished much over the years, and he travelled around the world to present lectures on the topic. Famous people visited him in his Winnipeg home, including former prime minister William Lyon Mackenzie King (who was known to regularly communicate with spirits, including his deceased dog) and Sir Arthur Conan Doyle, author of the Sherlock Holmes stories. Following his time spent with Dr. Hamilton, Doyle wrote, "Winnipeg stands very high among the places we have visited for its psychic possibilities."

MYSTERY IN THE MILL

Clyde River, Prince Edward Island

John Scott sat beside a small fire in his kitchen, desperately trying to soothe his tired and aching body. He was cold — so very cold — and nothing seemed to be able to warm his bones. He'd been sick for days and it was beginning to feel like he'd never get better. A cough from an adjoining room cut through the silence of the night. It was one of John's two children. But before he could check on them, his wife began yelling and moaning. She lay in bed on the second floor in a fevered state. The entire family was afflicted by the same illness, but none of the doctors who had tended to them could determine what it was.

Fear weighed heavily on John's mind as he listened to his family's pain and suffering. He was afraid of the unknown. He was afraid they might not recover. He was also afraid they would soon run out of money if he wasn't able to return to work; he owned and operated Scott's Mill, a gristmill with a reputation for making the best flour in the entire county. But now, thanks to the mysterious illness that had prevented him from working for days, large sacks of unground wheat filled the mill.

Suddenly a new sound filled the house. Not the rasping of his sick family, but a groan from the mill as it began grinding.

Adding the fear that someone had broken into the mill to his growing list of concerns, John wearily stood up. He put on his coat and hat and stepped out into the cold, dark night, then made his way down the steep hill between his house and the mill.

As he approached, he noticed the lantern that hung near the main entrance had been lit. He thought back to the last time he'd checked on the mill and knew he hadn't left the lantern lit, so he assumed whoever had broken in had done so. A thin wisp of flour dust floated in the air, visible in the beam of light cast by the lantern. The door was slightly ajar.

John searched the ground and picked up a thick, heavy stick. He twisted his hands over the rough bark, anger coursing through his veins. It was bad enough that someone had broken into his mill, but the fact that he had to deal with the intruder in his present state made him even more irritated. He was sick, his family was sick, their livelihood was in jeopardy and now someone was messing around with his mill. It was more than he could tolerate. It was more than he would allow.

Without hesitation John flung the door wide open and stepped quickly into the mill. The sight that met his eyes was so unexpected he froze and relaxed his grip on the stick.

The mill hadn't been vandalized or damaged in any way. On the contrary, it was in perfect shape. And not only that, but the mill was operating at peak capacity, the wheels spinning on their axles, the hopper filled with grain and the mouths of the elevators fitted snuggly with bags, ready to collect the freshly ground flour. A second light had been lit in the middle of the mill.

While John tried to make sense of it all, footsteps thudded down the creaky stairs. After a few seconds, John could finally see who was responsible for dragging him away from the comfort of the fire in his kitchen. It was a man whom John didn't recognize. As the man crossed the mill and ran his fingers through the grain he'd poured into the hopper, he didn't pay John any attention. It was as if he couldn't even see John. And his movements and actions proved he was an experienced hopper, but that raised even more questions. Not only why was he doing John's work for him, but where had he come from? John knew all the millers for a great distance around Clyde River, and this man was a complete mystery to him.

John opened his mouth to ask the man who he was but didn't have the chance. The door slammed shut with a terrible bang, the lanterns were blown out as if by invisible breath and the intruder disappeared into thin air. The wheels of the mill slowly came to a stop, and the entire building fell eerily silent.

Not one to scare easily, John reached into his pocket, pulled out a match, struck it, and held the flame to the extinguished lantern, lighting the room once more. John searched the entire mill, but the man was nowhere to be found. John knew then that the man hadn't been a man — not really — but a ghost, and his identity remains a mystery to this day.

Other strange and unexplainable things happened around Scott's Mill during those early days, but that was the only time John came face to face with the ghost. The family's health soon returned and the three bags of flour ground by the ghost helped them get through a tough time. But had John not interrupted the spirit's work, who can say how many bags he might have filled by sunrise.

THE CHILLS

Canmore, Alberta

It was a frigid November night in 1983, both outside and inside the Canmore Recreation Centre, but Kevin Stevenson, a hockey rink attendant, was used to the cold. His line of work wasn't well-suited for people who were prone to chills. But little did Kevin know that his blood was about to turn to ice — not from the temperature, but from something else entirely.

He was alone, driving the ice resurfacer around the rink, flooding it with a fresh layer of water. The hour was late and it was nearly quitting time, but Kevin's mind was focused on his work. All seemed normal, nothing was amiss, when a shiver suddenly shot up Kevin's spine. He had the terrible feeling he was no longer alone — that he was being watched. He stopped the tractor and scanned the ice. There was no one there. He looked at the players' benches, penalty boxes and stands. Not a soul. And then he looked to the top of the arena.

Staring at him from the booth was an unusual figure — someone very small, with extremely long hair. It was hard to tell from far away, but it appeared to be a young girl.

Kevin was so terrified by the girl's sudden appearance that he immediately started to cry. Tears flowed down his face nearly as steadily as the water had streamed from his vehicle only moments before. And then, without warning, the girl vanished.

Luckily Kevin didn't see the ghost girl again for some time. Unfortunately she didn't stay away forever. A few years later, Kevin was working in the arena's ice plant. Once again he was alone, but then the silence was broken by footsteps in the hallway. He stopped what he was doing and nervously opened the door, the memory of the long-haired watcher jumping out from the darkest depths of his mind — a place he'd hoped she would remain. There was no one in the hallway, but the footsteps continued.

Determined to find the source of the footsteps — if for no other reason than to prove there was a rational explanation for the sounds he was hearing — Kevin searched the rest of the arena and all of the change rooms, maintenance bays and offices. He even checked every corner of the dance hall that was also located in the recreation centre. There was no one there. He was certain he was completely alone. And yet the footsteps continued plodding through the building. The girl, Kevin knew, had returned.

Although he wanted to share his paranormal experiences with his co-workers, Kevin kept them to himself. He was afraid they'd laugh at him. He was convinced they'd tease him. But then one day, much to Kevin's relief, a colleague told him about an eerie experience he'd had that was shockingly similar to what Kevin had witnessed.

Tom Bisson had been alone late one night, working on the ice, when he'd suddenly felt eyes on the back of his neck. He looked up and spotted the ghost staring down at him from the same window where Kevin had first seen her. She was wispy and transparent, and looking at her made Tom feel terrible.

The two men had had similar experiences separately, and they were about to have an experience together. They were the only two people working in the recreation centre one night when they heard the girl calling for her mother.

"Mommy?" her soft voice called out. "Mommy?"

Over time Kevin and Tom learned they weren't the only two people who had seen the ghost either. A construction crew that was hired to work in the arena after-hours reported seeing her, and a maintenance staff supervisor's girlfriend saw her once too. Like Kevin, it took her a long time to build up the courage to share her story with anyone.

As more people opened up and talked about having heard or seen the girl, they also began to speculate about who she might be. Someone had heard that long before the recreation centre was built, a little girl had drowned in the swamp that once existed there. Her body was never discovered.

It's a haunting story that for many has made the building feel far chillier than it has any earthly reason to be. And it's impossible to say how many others have seen the girl with the long hair and have been too scared — too frozen — to ever tell a soul.

PEEKABOO

Whitehorse, Yukon

There was one room in Barbara Robertson's house that always gave her the creeps. She and her family moved into the small three-bedroom house at 406 Wood Street in downtown Whitehorse in 1965. Odd things began happening almost immediately, particularly in the baby's room.

One night as Barbara changed her daughter, Liz, the infant's attention was drawn to something behind her mother's back. It seemed to Barbara that the girl was looking at someone who had entered the room, so she spun around only to find the room empty. This happened again another night and another and another. It was always the same: Liz would see something and her eyes would grow wide, and yet every time Barbara turned to look, there was no one there.

As Liz grew up, she began to dislike the room. She no longer enjoyed playing there. It gave her a bad feeling. Specifically, she felt like someone was always watching her.

A few years later, Barbara's son, Douglas, had moved into the room. He was only ten months old the night Barbara woke up suddenly. She didn't know what had woken her; all she knew was that she felt a real and oppressive sense of horror. Something was very wrong, but what?

The sound of a small child laughing hysterically cut through the silence, then stopped. It was Douglas, laughing in his room. He started and stopped again and again as Barbara listened from her bed. What did he find so funny? It was as if someone was in the room with him, playing games and making the young boy giggle.

And then the memory of her daughter seeing someone only she could see — in that very room — came rushing back to Barbara.

She left the safety of her bed and crept through the darkened house to find out what was going on. She slapped her bare feet extra loudly on the floor to make sure that if someone was in the room with her son they would hear her coming.

She creaked the door open a crack and peeked inside. Douglas was standing up in his crib. He was smiling excitedly and pointing at the closet across the room. The closet door was open but no one was inside. Barbara often hid in the closet and poked her head out with a loud "peekaboo," which Douglas loved. He'd stand in his crib and laugh and point . . . just like he was doing at that moment. Although she couldn't see anyone hiding within the shadows of the closet, Barbara felt as though her son could. And whoever was hidden in there was playing peekaboo with the enthralled boy.

The Robertsons had purchased the house fully furnished from a family moving to South Africa, and they uncovered its history little by little. It was originally a log cabin first inhabited in 1906 by postmaster Dr. Frederick Warren Cane. Then, in the 1920s, it was owned by two riverboat captains, Campbell and McKay. As with many other heritage buildings in the same neighbourhood, it was named after one of its earliest and most famous inhabitants: in this case, it became known as the Captain Campbell House. Gordon Armstrong, a butcher, later moved into the house, and in 1950 he was elected as the first mayor of Whitehorse. Requiring a dedicated space to conduct his business affairs, he used one of the bedrooms as a personal office. But he never felt alone in that room. In fact he'd often look up from his work to see a young boy watching him or running through the walls. It was the very same room where Barbara's children had seen someone she could never see.

The story spread around the neighbourhood throughout the 1950s, and people began to believe the house was haunted by a young boy, seven or eight years old, who had drowned nearby during the previous decade.

Barbara and her family moved out in 1977. After twelve years living in Captain Campbell House, they'd had their fair share of creepy experiences.

Harold Ryder, whose family has owned the house for many years, told the Yukon Historical & Museums Association that a tourist had once rented the house for a few days. The tourist had not heard the ghostly tales about the house, and soon he not only saw, but also felt the ghost.

It was the end of a long day and the tourist was just beginning to fall asleep when someone tapped his shoulder. He rolled over just in time to catch sight of the ghost running out of the room. He was so scared that he bundled up some blankets and a pillow and marched straight outside. He slept on the front lawn that night.

Recently the house has sat empty and has fallen into disrepair. Many of the white pickets on the fence are broken or missing, some of the windows have been shattered and the front door is scuffed and weathered. It's been used for storage, not for living space. But one can't help but stand outside, peer into the darkness within, and wonder if a little boy is running from room to room, eternally playing peekaboo with the shadows.

THE FIRE WALKER

Dwight, Ontario

Ron Gostlin turned on the tap to add some water to a glass. He was serving one of his very first customers on the very first day he opened his new bar and nightclub in the Pine Grove Inn. But as soon as the glass neared the faucet, the water stopped flowing. Thinking that was odd, Ron placed the glass on the counter and leaned in to figure out what the issue was. The water started pouring again.

Ron shrugged, picked up the glass, and moved it back under the faucet. The water stopped again.

When the same action yielded the same result a third time, he took the glass into the back kitchen and filled it with water there. He'd heard the stories before he purchased the property, but this incident was Ron's first encounter with the Fire Walker, the ghost that has haunted the Pine Grove Inn since 1954.

Harry Corbett and his wife, Helen, built the Pine Grove Inn and opened it in 1906. At first it only had six guest rooms, but the Corbetts continued to expand the building. Soon the hotel could accommodate up to one hundred guests. They also built an ice cream parlour, a tennis court and the first garage for auto repairs in the area.

Helen handled all of the cooking, and her reputation spread far and wide. In the winter Harry kept the furnace stoked with coal and walked up and down the hallways every night to ensure each section of the hotel was warm enough to keep his guests comfortable. This chore was called "fire walking," and Harry was incredibly dedicated to the task, even after he suffered a fatal heart attack in 1954 as he walked up the second-floor staircase.

More than fifty years after Harry's death, on a cold January night not too long after the water tap incident, Ron was alone in the building.

Thump, thump. Thump, thump. Thump, thump.

It was the sound of footsteps from above. But all of the doors were locked and bolted, save for the front door, and Ron was standing near it — no one had passed him.

Thump, thump. Thump, thump. Thump, thump.

Whoever was up there was walking back and forth.

Thump, thump. Thump, thump. Thump, thump.

Up and down the second-floor hallway.

I'm hearing things, Ron thought. *My mind is playing tricks on me.*

Somehow he gathered the courage to go and investigate. There hadn't been power on the second or third floors since he'd purchased the property, so he picked up a flashlight, turned it on, and made his way slowly upstairs. As soon as he reached the stairs where Harry had died, the footsteps stopped. Everything appeared to be normal, until Ron reached the hallway at the top of the stairs and pointed his flashlight at the floor in front of him.

His light reflected off small puddles of water — wet footprints that led from the bathroom down the length of the hallway. Ron couldn't believe his eyes. He continued his search and confirmed there was absolutely no one else in the building other than him, but what made the wet footprints even harder to believe was that the water pipes on the second floor hadn't been connected for more than two years.

After annoying and scaring Ron, the ghost was about to become much more dangerous. Early one morning Ron stepped outside and made his way to the shed. He was carrying his keys, a clipboard, some pens, a drink and a flashlight. The shed had been modified to contain a walk-in cooler, and he was going to take inventory. The flashlight he was carrying was of the utmost importance because the lights in the shed hadn't worked since long before he'd bought the property. He'd hired two electricians but neither had been able to figure out what the problem was, so without the flashlight he wouldn't be able to see what he was doing.

Ron fumbled to get the key into the lock, and as soon as he unlocked the door, an unseen presence violently knocked everything out of his hands, sending his possessions flying through the air.

Something inside of Ron snapped. He'd had enough of the Fire Walker's antics.

"Harry!" he shouted. "Turn these lights on!"

Without a moment's delay, all the shed lights turned on — the same lights that hadn't worked in years.

Ron was astounded.

"Thank you, Harry," he said, in shock.

Harry continued to haunt the Pine Grove Inn, but Ron discovered that if he was polite to the spirit, Harry wasn't quite as troublesome as he'd been before. And so, from then on, Ron would begin each day by wishing Harry a good morning, and he'd end each day by wishing him good night.

Ron no longer operates the bar. Pine Grove Inn is now Corbett Cove Villas, an upscale vacation destination. It's not known whether the Fire Walker continues to roam the property after nightfall, but guests are encouraged to mind their manners, just in case. After all, if you're rude in Harry's presence, you're playing with fire.

IN THE SPIRIT ZONE

Yellowknife, Northwest Territories

Kevin Dunbar, a drummer in a Yellowknife band, was alone in a rehearsal space near Kam Lake. It was midnight, and Kevin was tired after a long day jamming. The rest of the band had already gone home and Kevin was looking forward to doing the same.

But when Kevin looked up, he discovered he was no longer alone. There was a teenaged boy standing in the doorway, scowling at him. Before Kevin could do or say anything, the boy made an aggressive move toward him, bared his teeth like a dog, and growled, then turned and ran down the hall. Startled, Kevin chased after the angry youth . . . only to find the hall was empty. The boy was gone. It was as if he had disappeared into thin air.

It was the incident that pushed Kevin over the edge.

There had been plenty of other odd experiences in the rehearsal space over the years, which led to people whispering that the old building might be haunted, but Kevin hadn't put any stock in the rumours before. Now, having come face to face with a ghost, Kevin believed.

The rehearsal space was located where Bevan's Dairy Farm had operated in the late 1950s. The farm was short-lived, and so were the cows. Back then they were led to Kam Lake to drink, but the water was contaminated by arsenic discharged from a nearby mine. After all the cows died, the dairy farm closed and a hodgepodge of industrial buildings, dog kennels and residential homes were built in the area over the years, turning Kam Lake into one of the more colourful neighbourhoods of the city. The haunted rehearsal space has added to the uniqueness of the neighbourhood, but the fact that it's haunted shouldn't come as a surprise. At least not according to a medium who was brought in to investigate the situation shortly after the ghost boy appeared and disappeared before Kevin's eyes.

The visions were becoming too regular and the activity too unnerving, and it was believed the medium might be able to help whatever spirits were trapped in the building and clear out the weird energy. Almost immediately she picked up on a teenage presence, which she described as being mischievous but harmless. And she wasn't at all surprised the building was haunted. She believed musicians have the ability — whether they know it or not — to intercept wayward spirits when they're in the zone and thoroughly engaged in their music.

Perhaps that's why the ghost had settled there, but

hearing that — or the fact that the medium felt the spirit was harmless — didn't give Kevin any comfort. He and others felt the ghost wasn't harmless at all, but evil. They saw black shadows floating through the halls, an ominous sighting that never failed to make the hair on the back of their necks stand up. Sensing the paranormal energy was such a gut-churning experience that Kevin was always overcome by the desire to leave the building immediately. But that wasn't always possible, such as those times his band was actively recording.

One night, when the band was deep in the zone and their jam was going particularly well, something very peculiar interrupted them. The teen boy didn't appear — neither in his full form nor as a shadow — but he did make his presence known. Kevin was on the drums in front of their control board. To his left was a table, and on top of it lay an iPod. Suddenly Kevin saw the iPod flip 180 degrees in the air and land back on the table screen-down. No one was standing close to it, nothing had been touching it and there hadn't been any cords plugged into it that might have been yanked or pulled accidentally. There was no explanation for what had happened. Kevin and the band were certain the ghost had joined their practice once again.

One thing is clear: Kevin's band's sessions are music to the ghost's ears. Although they would rather play for a live audience, the band will have to settle for playing to an audience of the dead.

THE OLD HAG

St. John's, Newfoundland and Labrador

It seemed like a normal evening in March of 1998. A young woman readied for bed, turned out the light, and fell asleep. She had never experienced anything odd or unusual in Sutherland Place, where she rented an apartment in the attic, so she had no way to anticipate what was to happen in the middle of the night.

She slept peacefully for a few hours, but then something from her dreams woke her from her deep slumber. Although she couldn't recall what she'd been dreaming about, she was overcome by the feeling she was no longer alone. Worse than that, she feared that whoever — or whatever — had come for her intended to harm her.

Resisting the urge to pull her bedsheet over her head and hide, she sat up, hoping to find the room empty.

Sutherland Place

It wasn't. The ghost of an old woman was at the foot of the bed, looming over her. The ghost had long dark hair, and the black dress she wore seemed to flow around her withered body. How long had she been in the room, silently watching, filled with hatred?

The young woman screamed at the top of her lungs, leapt out of her bed, sprinted past the old woman, and ran into the bedroom of her roommate. She was too scared to return to her own room for the rest of the night.

Upon hearing this story, there were some who felt they knew who the old woman was: the Old Hag. Some say she's the ghost of a nameless witch. She's been known to haunt people's dreams throughout the province. Over the years countless people have woken in the middle of the night with the sinking feeling they're being watched. And then they see her — in the room, standing at the foot of the bed, sometimes sitting on the victim's chest. And when she sits on top of someone, they can't move. They can't scream. They can hardly breathe. Luckily for the woman who ran out of her room in terror, the Old Hag didn't get close enough to pin her down.

The Old Hag seems to be fond of Sutherland Place. Built on King's Bridge Road in 1883, the building was originally the home of the Honourable James S. Pitts and was converted into an apartment building in 1924. It has been the home of many of the province's most distinguished (and haunted) community members.

In the middle of the night not too long after the encounter in the attic, another woman returned home to Sutherland Place. Her apartment was beside the other woman's, but she hadn't yet heard about the paranormal activity. She worked in a pub, so she was used to getting home late, and neither the dark nor the quiet bothered her. She opened the door, locked it behind her with a *click*, and walked down the hallway toward her bedroom. As she passed the living room, her heart stopped for a second.

There was an old woman with long black hair and a flowing black dress sitting alone in the shadows.

The bartender didn't stop to ask who the old woman was. She hurried to her bedroom and woke up her boyfriend. She demanded to know who the stranger sitting in the living room was. He insisted the apartment was empty. He got out of bed, and together they searched the entire apartment. The doors and windows were all locked. They looked in every nook and cranny, but there was no one there. The Old Hag had disappeared.

The most terrifying was yet to come.

The next month a woman named Michelle sublet a room in one of the attic apartments. Neither of the women who already lived in that part of the building told Michelle what had happened.

During her first night in Sutherland Place, Michelle woke with a start. She sat up straight and struggled to control her breathing. She was covered in sweat and her sheets were soaked. She didn't see anyone else in her room, but Michelle had the odd sensation that something wasn't right, that she wasn't alone. For the next few days, she often felt a disquieting presence in the apartment, and it was often quiet . . . too quiet. Like something was sucking all sound — even white noise like the hum of electricity or the thrum of the furnace — out of the very air.

A few days later, Michelle was sitting on the living-room couch, talking on the phone with a friend. She was alone. Without warning, the couch began rocking violently back and forth. Michelle cut her telephone conversation short, jumped off the shaking couch, and looked for the source of the disturbance. The room was completely empty.

The following week Michelle was in the north staircase on her way to work. It was early in the morning and her mood was bright, thanks in part to the new outfit she was wearing. But then, without warning, Michelle felt a hand shove her hard from behind. She flew off her feet and tumbled down the last flight of stairs. She landed on the floor and looked up to see who had attacked her without provocation. There was no one there. Although her new pants had been ruined and she was in a great deal of pain, Michelle felt she was lucky she hadn't been seriously injured. But the phantom push was her tipping point; she left the apartment and refused to return on her own, returning only briefly later to retrieve her belongings with the assistance — and safety — of a friend.

The Old Hag clearly wanted Michelle out of the building, but the small victory hasn't been enough to sate the ghost. More reports of paranormal activity in Sutherland Place have surfaced in the years since, and the Old Hag continues to terrorize people after they've fallen asleep. You can try to stay awake, but sooner or later you're going to nod off. And when your eyes are closed, your body is resting and your mind is dreaming peacefully, the Old Hag is creeping closer and closer and closer . . .

WATCHING OVER THEM

Egan-Sud, Quebec

James Maloney was hard at work grinding grain into flour in his gristmill on the Desert River. Although it was early spring and the sun was shining, winter hadn't given up the ghost yet and the air was still cold enough to chill the bones of the heartiest of people. But it was warm in the mill, and James was so focused on his job that he hadn't taken note of the weather. For the better part of the past year, he'd thrown himself at his work, cutting out many things that had previously brought him joy in order not to think of his wife, Corabella, who had died suddenly in the spring of 1859.

A sudden thought popped into James's head, breaking his dogged concentration: he hadn't seen Dorothy or Diane, his two daughters, in quite some time. The girls were only four and six years old, so James couldn't leave them in their secluded, picturesque house — which he and Corabella had built by a small waterfall — while he worked all day. And so the girls had become very familiar with the gristmill and its surroundings, although they were warned never to venture too far away on their own. But it was soon discovered they had disobeyed that rule and wandered into the woods.

Overcome by panic, James ran through the settlement yelling and calling for his daughters. He couldn't lose Dorothy and Diane — he'd already been through too much, suffered too deeply. If something unthinkable had happened to his girls . . . he might never recover.

When word of the disappearance reached Patrick Moore, a foreman at a lumber camp nearly five kilometres from the gristmill, he immediately organized a search party. Among Patrick's team were Tom Budge, Moses Leary, Robert Carney, William Tarrney and John Michel — all of them experienced woodsmen who knew the area well and were trained to track animals with much smaller prints than two lost girls. If anyone could find James's daughters, it would be them.

But spirits sank as days passed without finding the girls. The team picked up the girls' trail north along the Desert River, then again for eight kilometres along the Eagle River. Their footprints dotted the riverbanks, and the search party found signs of where they had curled up one night beneath the thick roots of an old tree, then another night beneath a blanket of collected leaves. The men were such expert trackers they even found signs of how the girls were surviving in the woods, spotting areas where they'd eaten wintergreen berries and wild rosehip.

Soon it had been a week since the girls had disappeared, and the men still hadn't found them. Their trail meandered in a haphazard fashion, along sandy beaches, through thick bush and up and down hillsides, causing the men to occasionally lose track of them. But each time the search party began to lose hope, someone caught sight of a telltale sign and the hunt was back on.

"Someone must be watching over them," Patrick Moore said one morning, in an astonished but solemn tone. It was cold and wet, and although no one suggested quitting the search, it wouldn't be surprising if the thought had entered at least one or two of their heads. "They are still alive. Let us not give up."

An eighth day passed, then a ninth. The men found the occasional trail of footprints or some other sign, but still not the girls themselves.

"Dorothy?" the men called. "Diane? Where are you?"

There was never a reply, only their own voices echoing from the surrounding hills.

After the tenth day since the girls' disappearance, a few of the men openly doubted they were still alive. One or two suggested calling off the search and returning home.

Patrick wouldn't hear it. "Someone must be watching over them," he said again, a phrase he'd repeated more than once over the course of the previous few days.

"I believe they are still alive," John Michel said, backing up Patrick. "It seems like a miracle but the signs say they are still alive."

John's words held a lot of weight with the doubters of the group. He knew the area better than anyone and he was the most-skilled tracker among them. If he still had hope, they should too. They carried on.

But then, on the fourteenth day, the girls' trail led the party to a great swamp on the shore of Cedar Lake.

"No one can stay alive in there for very long," one of the men said.

No one disagreed. It was a dangerous and inhospitable place and nearly impossible to safely traverse.

All of the men decided to disband and seek shelter and food at a nearby lumber camp before heading back home in the morning, defeated. All, that is, except for one.

"I believe they are still alive," John said, more to himself than to the others. "I know the swamp well. I will go on alone."

The next morning, two weeks and a day after the girls had wandered away from their father's gristmill, John spotted something moving through the trees ahead. *Two* somethings — the girls! They were cold, hungry and terrified beyond belief, but alive.

When asked how they'd survived so long without any provisions, Dorothy mumbled, "It was the Woman in White."

John was perplexed by that response, but it was obvious the girls had been through a terrible ordeal. If they were a little dazed and confused, who could blame them? He took off his jacket and wrapped them both in it, then picked them up and carried them out of the swamp and through the wilderness to the lumber camp.

Some of the other men from the search party were still there, preparing to return home, when John appeared with Dorothy and Diane on his back.

"It was the Woman in White who saved us," Dorothy repeated to everyone who asked how they'd survived so long alone. Hard as it was to believe, her story still hadn't changed by the time they were safely returned home to their grateful father.

"How did she do that?" James asked once he'd finally recovered enough to form proper sentences, not knowing what to believe but too relieved to care.

"Every night she stood by us in the forest when we lay down to sleep and watched over us," Dorothy said.

"She looked just like Mother," Diane added, with a sincere nod. "And she was all in white, just like an angel."

That was enough to turn James into an ardent believer in the afterlife. He was convinced that the Woman in White was the ghost of his late wife, Corabella. And Dorothy and Diane's tale of supernatural survival was passed down from generation to generation, turning the Woman in White into the most famous of the Gatineau ghosts.

FRIGHT IN THE FORT

Toronto, Ontario

It was a cold night, and the fort was quiet and still. A group of Girl Guides was having a sleepover in Fort York, and everyone was asleep in the barracks when one girl was woken by her bunk mate. She needed to use the bathroom, and since it was located in another building, they had been told to buddy up and go in pairs.

It was late April and still cold enough outside to chatter teeth and rattle bones. The ground was covered by a blanket of knee-high mist that shone in the moonlight and swirled around the girls' legs, leaving a wake behind them. They were both already creeped out by the moody atmosphere of the night when they spotted a man and stopped dead in their tracks.

Dressed in an old-fashioned military uniform, which

included a red jacket, and holding a musket against his shoulder, he stood at attention, staring toward Lake Ontario. Although he wasn't too far away, the soldier didn't seem to notice the girls at all. He gave the girls the creeps and made them feel very uneasy, so they hurried along to the bathroom.

Being tired, cold and now scared, the girls were in and out of the bathroom in record time. They wanted to return to the warmth and safety of their beds immediately. But that didn't happen. They both paused. The soldier was gone. The girls scanned the grounds. He was nowhere to be seen. Then one of the girls, her heart pounding in her chest, pointed out that the mist where the man had stood was still and undisturbed. They raced each other back to the barracks, the mist swirling as they ran, proving to them they weren't overreacting. The soldier should have left a trail in the mist. They could think of only one logical explanation: the soldier was a ghost.

Instead of lying in separate beds, the girls shared one. They didn't sleep all night, huddling together and shaking until sunrise.

This happened in 1996, the same year a group of teen-aged boys in the Canadian Cadet Program also had a sleepover in the Fort York barracks. After a long, tiring day, they were trying to get a little shut-eye when something happened that kept their eyes wide with fear the rest of the night. After a few hours of sleep, they woke to see a woman in a long, flowing dress slowly approaching their beds, her arms outstretched and her hands opening and closing as if she wanted to lead them away. Scared to death, the boys sat up in their beds and screamed. The woman disappeared.

Neither group knew it at the time, but they'd both had encounters with the two ghosts most commonly seen in Fort York. Little is known about who they might be, but most people agree it's likely they were casualties of the Battle of York. Fought on April 27, 1813, during the War of 1812, the battle claimed the lives of nearly 500 people. In the years following, people started noticing that the frequency of creepy experiences intensified in the days leading up to the anniversary of the battle.

Doors slammed shut on their own. Doorknobs rattled as if something on the other side was trying to get in. Curtains flew up and down. Heavy footsteps clomped

A soldier at Fort York

through empty rooms. Invisible hands pushed and pulled. In terms of classic signs of a haunting, Fort York has it all, and there is no shortage of reports from people — like the young Guides and cadets — who have seen a fully formed ghost . . . or two . . . or more.

Between 1977 and 1980 Robin Shepherd worked in Fort York's kitchen and experienced many unusual events. One of the kitchen doors would often open and shut on its own while she was working alone, followed a moment later by the door at the opposite end of the kitchen opening and closing as well; it was as if an invisible presence had casually strolled through. If the fort's two cats, Mrs. Simcoe and Fred, were nearby when the doors opened and closed, their claws would come out, they'd hiss and then they'd dart off as fast as lightning. Guides and maintenance staff often told Robin they had seen ghosts in old military uniforms — both British and American — wandering aimlessly around the grounds or standing at attention as the flags were raised and lowered. And she herself once saw a ghost staring out a window on the second floor of the block house when the building was completely empty.

In the winter of 1998, a man was walking around the grounds with his dog when he noticed another man leaning against a tree, silently watching him from fifty metres away. Something about the stranger gave the man a bad feeling. He turned to look at his car, and when he turned back around, the stranger had vanished. The man hurried to the tree and looked up into the branches — it was the only place the stranger could have hidden so quickly — but he wasn't there. Not only that, but there were no footprints in the snow other than his own. The man rushed to his car and went straight home. His wife immediately knew something was wrong. He told her he had considered himself to be a skeptic when it came to the paranormal, but his experience at Fort York had changed his mind forever.

A staff member who had locked up one night in 2003 was walking toward the front gate when he noticed a light on in the officers' quarters. Reluctantly, he turned and walked back to the building, realizing something odd: there wasn't a light in that part of the building. As he neared the quarters, he saw shadows moving inside. They were the silhouettes of men and women — a complete dinner party — walking, talking and dancing. As he continued on his way, the people gradually disappeared and the light dimmed. By the time he reached the door, the dinner party had vanished and the light was completely extinguished. He didn't bother entering the building but turned and hurried away without another look back over his shoulder.

Perhaps the most dramatic paranormal encounter at Fort York happened in the summer of 2013. A woman who wanted to visit the fort was a little late after getting stuck in traffic. The upside was she was allowed in for free since it was nearly closing time, but it wasn't worth the sight that met her eyes in the middle of the fort. First a sixth sense warned her she was in danger. Next she smelled gunpowder and burning flesh. Then she saw soldiers in red uniforms all around her, moaning, screaming, bleeding and dying. Finally the vision suddenly disappeared. Needless to say the woman was incredibly distraught, and she cut her visit short.

With so many reports of shell-shocked visitors and staff over the years, it seems old wounds will never heal in the historic Fort York.

DON'T GET CAUGHT

Regina, Saskatchewan

It was a hot summer day, and friends Howard and Mike were chasing two other buddies around Howard's backyard. The boys, none above the age of nine, were obsessed with *Starsky & Hutch*, a popular 1970s television show about a pair of police detectives. During this particular game, Howard and Mike were pretending to be the heroes while the other two were the criminals.

The chase wound dangerously around Howard's swing set — one misstep could send them face first into the rusty metal frame. So when their two friends slowed down, Howard and Mike closed the gap. Sensing he was about to be caught, one of the "criminals" tossed the item he'd "stolen," Mike's tennis shoe, high into the air. The shoe sailed over Howard's back fence, across the alley behind his house, and into his neighbour's backyard.

Mike's heart sank as he watched his shoe disappear from view. He'd removed both shoes before the game because they were brand new and his parents would be upset if he let them get covered in grass stains. Obviously he couldn't return home with only one shoe. That would be worse than returning with two dirtied shoes. But retrieving the tossed shoe wasn't going to be easy.

The shoe had been thrown directly into the Bat Lady's yard.

The boys abandoned their game and sat down on the grass to discuss their options, well aware that their options weren't great. They couldn't ask Howard's mother for help. She was known for two things: her generosity with Popsicles and her strict enforcement of certain playtime rules, chief among them that the boys could be as rambunctious as they liked as long as they didn't disturb the neighbours. So she wouldn't be sympathetic to their current predicament. And they couldn't simply knock on the front door and ask for the Bat Lady's help. They'd already had several bad encounters with her over the years, often when caught trying to retrieve a baseball that had been hit into her yard. The boys called her the Bat Lady because she always dressed in black from head to toe, and when she chased them from her yard, she shrieked and flapped her arms like giant leathery wings.

The only thing any of the boys could think to do was to sneak into her yard and hope for the best. Maybe the Bat Lady was out. Maybe she was having an afternoon nap. Maybe they wouldn't get caught. Maybe . . .

Howard, the boys all agreed, was the strongest climber, so he was chosen for the job. His heart pounded in his chest as he crossed the alley and paused in front of the Bat Lady's fence. The fence boards were tall and warped, weathered by many years of sun and snow. The true challenge wasn't climbing the fence to enter the yard, but climbing the fence to leave; it was one thing to complete the task with all the time in the world, and another to do it with someone chasing you while lobbing curses and threats at your back.

Peering between the boards, Howard spied the shoe. It had landed beside some sad-looking tomatoes in the Bat Lady's garden. He might need to run through the vegetable garden to save time, which would no doubt enrage the Bat Lady even more than running across her yellow grass, but that couldn't be helped. At least the shoe was near the fence instead of the house, buying him a little time.

And then Howard noticed something else — something he had never noticed before — that made him feel better still about his odds of success. There was a rickety gate at the far end of the fence, camouflaged by the ramshackle state of the fence as a whole. It had a lift-and-pull latch above the handle and wasn't secured with a lock, so he'd be able to exit the backyard that much quicker without needing to climb the fence on his way out.

This will be easy, Howard thought, as he stepped onto a garbage can to get over the fence, not realizing how wrong he could be.

He hopped over the fence and landed awkwardly, twisting his right ankle. He yelled and stood up quickly, testing his ankle to see if he could put any weight on it. It hurt but not bad enough to stop him, so he hurried to the garden. Howard bent to pick up Mike's tennis shoe and noticed it was suddenly flanked by two others, a pair of beaten-up black shoes. Wearing the pair of black shoes was the Bat Lady. Howard looked up in terror and was met by her piercing dark eyes staring down at him sternly.

He'd never been so close to her before, and he wished with all his might that he wasn't so close to her now. Her hair was matted and unwashed. Her skin was wrinkled and dirty. She had no teeth, and her body was nothing but skin and bones. She stared at Howard and raised a gnarled finger at him accusingly, and the boy was filled with dread at what she might do next. He didn't wait to find out. He turned and ran as if his life depended on reaching the gate before the Bat Lady.

She yelled and mumbled and cursed him as he ran. Her fingers tugged on the back of his shirt, and although Howard was amazed that the old woman was quick enough to keep up with him, he didn't dare turn around to look at her. He picked up his pace, broke free from her grasp, reached the gate in record time, opened the latch, and pulled with all his might.

But the gate didn't budge. It was stuck in the earth. It clearly hadn't been opened for years, if not decades. Like a fly in a spider's web, he was trapped.

Howard turned around to face his fate and gasped.

The Bat Lady was gone.

Her backyard was empty. But that didn't make any sense. The yard was too big and the house too far away for her to have made it back inside, and there was nowhere else she could have hidden from view. Plus, why would she have left before teaching Howard a lesson for trespassing on her property? The unanswered questions piling up in his head frightened him even more than the threat of the Bat Lady catching him had. He decided it would be better to figure things out from the safety of his own backyard. Howard found an empty milk crate and used it to step high enough to grab the top of the fence and pull himself out to safety.

The other three boys were desperate to hear what had happened and why Howard had taken so long to return. Once he'd caught his breath and calmed his nerves, he told them everything. But they didn't seem to believe him. For starters they hadn't heard a sound the entire time he'd been gone, and the Bat Lady was usually loud enough to be heard a few streets away in every direction. Plus, why had Howard entered her backyard if she was already outside? He couldn't explain that, other than to insist she hadn't been standing in the garden when he climbed over the fence. But if that was so, how had she appeared so suddenly, as if out of thin air?

Howard felt like he was going to be sick. The others wanted more details, but Howard couldn't stomach any more of their questions. He gave Mike his shoe and said he needed to go inside. He went straight to his bedroom, where he remained hidden until his mother called him to dinner.

Although he wasn't hungry, he pecked away at his food, his sole goal being to finish enough to be allowed to leave the table. He barely said a word and hardly registered what his parents and sister, Wendy, discussed. Something about the police being called to their neighbourhood late the night before, and then something about an unfortunate person who had made a gruesome discovery. Howard pushed food around his plate and wondered if he'd made enough of a dent, his mind preoccupied by the Bat Lady and trying to figure out how she'd disappeared as suddenly as she'd appeared.

"How *long* had she been there?" Wendy asked their parents. "Were there any bugs?"

If either of his parents answered his sister's odd questions — questions that made no sense to him at the time — Howard didn't hear. He took one more bite and went back to his room.

Wendy walked into his room a couple of hours later and rapped on the door to get his attention. Normally Howard would have complained about her not knocking *before* entering, but that night he didn't care. He was still too preoccupied by what had happened that afternoon to be bothered by anything else, and he tried to put his mind at ease by bouncing a small rubber ball off the wall. It was obvious that Wendy was bursting with something she wanted to tell him, and it didn't seem to matter that Howard wasn't interested; she practically tripped over her words in an effort to get them out as quickly as possible.

She'd overheard their parents talking in the den after dinner.

"There were bugs," she said, with morbid curiosity and a healthy dose of disgust. "There had to have been. Dad said he figured she had been there for days and days, maybe more than a week, before anyone found her."

When Howard didn't comment, Wendy asked him if he didn't think that the whole thing was gross. He told her he had no idea what she was talking about.

"Where were you at dinner?" she asked incredulously. "Do you ever listen to anyone?"

Howard shrugged and bounced his ball against the wall one more time.

"That old woman across the alley," Wendy shouted. "She's *dead*! She's been dead for ages, but no one found her until last night." Without waiting for Howard to respond, Wendy left the room and slammed the door.

Howard dropped his ball. A sudden shiver seized his body, chilling his blood and making him wish he wasn't alone.

Howard's friends asked him to come out and play the following day, but Howard turned them down without explanation. He didn't dare enter his own backyard for several more days, and he never went anywhere near the Bat Lady's house, not even after a new family moved in. They completely renovated the house, including the backyard, replacing the old wooden fence with a metal chain-link fence. With care and attention, the grass turned green again and the garden returned to a healthy state.

But Howard wasn't the same. His friends asked him for more information about what had happened when he'd been alone in the Bat Lady's backyard. Howard said nothing. It took him twenty years before he was able to share the story with anyone.

Photo credit: Colleen Morris

Joel A. Sutherland is an author and librarian. He is the author of several books in the Haunted Canada series, as well as *Be a Writing Superstar, Summer's End* and Haunted, a series of middle-grade horror novels. His short fiction has appeared in many anthologies and magazines, alongside the likes of Stephen King and Neil Gaiman. He has been a juror for the John Spray Mystery Award and the Monica Hughes Award for Science Fiction and Fantasy.

He appeared as "The Barbarian Librarian" on the Canadian edition of the hit television show *Wipeout,* making it all the way to the third round and proving that librarians can be just as tough and crazy as anyone else.

Joel lives with his family in southeastern Ontario, where he is always on the lookout for ghosts.